Teaching in Tandem

Teaching in Tandem

Effective Co-Teaching in the Inclusive Classroom

Gloria Lodato Wilson
Joan Blednick

Alexandria, Virginia USA

1703 N. Beauregard St. • Alexandria, VA 22311-1714 USA
Phone: 800-933-2723 or 703-578-9600 • Fax: 703-575-5400
Website: www.ascd.org • E-mail: member@ascd.org
Author guidelines: www.ascd.org/write

Gene R. Carter, *Executive Director;* Judy Zimny, *Chief Program Development Officer;* Gayle Owens, *Managing Director, Content Acquisitions and Development;* Scott Willis, *Director, Book Acquisitions & Development;* Laura Lawson, *Acquisitions Editor;* Julie Houtz, *Director, Book Editing & Production;* Darcie Russell, *Senior Associate Editor;* Sima Nasr, *Senior Graphic Designer;* Mike Kalyan, *Production Manager;* Valerie Younkin, *Desktop Publishing Specialist*

Printed in the United States of America. Cover art © 2011 by ASCD. ASCD publications present a variety of viewpoints. The views expressed or implied in this book should not be interpreted as official positions of the Association.

All web links in this book are correct as of the publication date below but may have become inactive or otherwise modified since that time. If you notice a deactivated or changed link, please e-mail books@ascd.org with the words "Link Update" in the subject line. In your message, please specify the web link, the book title, and the page number on which the link appears.

Figures 5.2 and 5.3 ©2010 by Lee Ann Jung, Thomas R. Guskey. Reprinted courtesy of Jung, L. A., & Guskey, T. R. (2010). Grading exceptional learners. *Educational Leadership, 65*(5), 31–35.

PAPERBACK ISBN: 978-1-4166-1340-4 ASCD product #110029   n12/11
Also available as an e-book (see Books in Print for the ISBNs).

Quantity discounts for the paperback edition only: 10–49 copies, 10%; 50+ copies, 15%; for 1,000 or more copies, call 800-933-2723, ext. 5634, or 703-575-5634. For desk copies: member@ascd.org.

Library of Congress Cataloging-in-Publication Data
Wilson, Gloria Lodato.
  Teaching in tandem : effective co-teaching in the inclusive classroom / Gloria Lodato Wilson and Joan Blednick.
    p. cm.
  Includes bibliographical references and index.
  ISBN 978-1-4166-1340-4 (pbk. : alk. paper) 1. Teaching teams—United States. 2. Inclusive education—United States. 3. Mainstreaming in education—United States. I. Blednick, Joan. II. Title.
  LB1029.T4.W55 2011
  371.14'8—dc23
                                                                2011032296

20 19 18 17 16 15   2 3 4 5 6 7 8 9 10 11 12

Teaching in Tandem:

Effective Co-Teaching in the Inclusive Classroom

Introduction

We just don't know was the response to the question *What can we expect from this child?* The year was 1972. The question was posed to a doctor holding a young child with special needs during the exposé of Staten Island's Willowbrook State School (Primo, 1972). How did anyone know the capabilities of children who were not exposed to any typical conditions of life, including basic hygiene and social interactions? Today, with the advantages of decades of federal and state legislation, research, and the devoted practices and advocacy of educators and families, life for a child with special needs is quite different than it was in the 1970s.

But we still have the same answer to the same question: *What can we expect from this child? We don't know.* And we won't know unless we relentlessly push ourselves to remember that all children are entitled to experience the rhythms and conditions of life that most of us enjoy (Wolfensberger, 1972), including an education at a neighborhood school, in typical classes, with highly qualified teachers who are teaching standard curricula.

To reach that goal, schools are adopting the practice of co-teaching. Simply defined, co-teaching is the pairing of a general education teacher and a special education teacher in a classroom filled with diverse learners. We've seen it work. We've seen students with special needs thrive in classrooms where co-teachers create amazing opportunities for learning.

Admittedly, the stakes are high. Learning doesn't automatically happen when two teachers are put in a classroom. If co-teaching is done poorly, instead of getting more intensive instruction, increased opportunities to learn, and reduced stigma, students with special needs get just the opposite. Having experienced many successful co-taught classes, we are committed to supporting those co-teachers who are striving and succeeding in their quest to improve the teaching and learning of all students. Co-teaching is difficult and complex and dependent on a host of interwoven conditions (Friend, Cook, Hurley-Chamberlain, & Shamberger, 2010), but success in a co-taught inclusive class for many students with special needs is eminently possible.

As with any educational setting, there is a wide variance in co-teaching techniques, and it's typical for administrators, teachers, students, and parents to have questions about the program. *What does it look like? How does it work? Is it effective? Why are we doing this? Are we doing this right?* Answers to these questions are crucial to the effectiveness of the program, yet most of the questions are rarely satisfactorily answered and may be baffling to practitioners. Although some teachers and administrators may attend workshops, seminars, and college courses on co-teaching, the professional development on co-teaching is often haphazard. Teachers and administrators are involved in the program one year, but not the next; groups of teachers or administrators are trained one year, but the next group may not be given the same access to information or training. Other educators may be just interested in co-teaching but don't know where to find helpful information.

Administrators, teachers, and parents have asked where they can find reader-friendly information on co-teaching. And, now, we're giving you (and them) the answer. *Teaching in Tandem: Effective Co-Teaching in the Inclusive Classroom* gives concise and informative answers to a comprehensive array of critical questions and provides a much-needed resource for teachers, administrators, parents, and paraprofessionals. Written in a question-and-answer format, readers can quickly learn about the components of co-teaching. The questions are authentic, culled from the queries of active teachers and administrators, as well as from preservice teachers and parents. The information is useful to those already involved in co-teaching programs who want to make the programs more effective, and to those yet to embark on the effort. We will describe co-teaching, show you how to solve problems when new areas of difficulties arise, and provide you with a range of knowledge and tools. We've included short case studies about issues common to co-teaching situations for you to use in starting conversations and brainstorming your own solutions to day-to-day problems inherent to many co-teaching programs. In addition, each chapter addresses important and essential co-teaching components and includes voices from those involved in co-teaching programs—both positive and negative responses—as we work to dispel myths and build the scaffolds for an equitable education for all students.

I know my child has significant learning problems but I want her to have as typical a life as others. That means having high expectations and being in classes with the kids from the neighborhood.

—*A parent of a child with learning disabilities*

It's taken me a while and it's a complex program but I'm seeing the benefits to all kids in the co-teaching classes. The co-teachers are really able to differentiate instruction to everyone in the class.

—*An elementary school principal*

In September, it was very overwhelming but my co-teacher and I kept trying different ways of getting the students to learn and behave. By June the students with disabilities were thriving. This experience made us realize how important it is to give students with special needs a chance in a general education class.

—*A general education elementary co-teacher*

Sometimes I really wonder if we are doing the right thing with co-teaching. I don't feel that we really address the learning needs of the students and maybe they could learn a lot more if they were in segregated settings. On a social level, I support inclusive co-teaching classes, but on an academic level I don't think the students can keep up.

—*A special education elementary co-teacher*

1

Understanding the Basics

Ms. Bell, the middle school special education supervisor, is talking to the parent of a student (Ramond) in the self-contained class (a substantially separate, segregated class for students with disabilities) about the benefits of learning in an inclusive, co-taught setting. Ms. Bell knows that even 5 years ago she wouldn't have been having this conversation with this particular parent. But co-teaching has been established in the middle school, and teams of teachers have become more adept at understanding the diverse needs of students, as well as their often invisible strengths. Ms. Bell believes the time is right to include students with challenging learning needs in general education classes. Ramond's mother seems a bit apprehensive but hopeful; Ms. Bell knows that it will take true collaboration among the teachers, the parent, and the administration to support this new placement. In fact, this afternoon, Ms. Bell is meeting with the 6th grade team to discuss Ramond's transition into the inclusive, co-taught classes.

The 6th grade teaching team listens as Ms. Bell details the plan for Ramond to begin attending and learning in their classes. The teaching team is Ms. Rider,

5

special education; Ms. Simpson, social studies and language arts; Mr. Ross, science; and Ms. Levin, math. They have been working together for three years and they see how beneficial co-teaching is for all students. They listen as Ms. Bell describes Ramond. Yes, he does have difficulties with basic reading and writing skills, along with struggles in understanding and remembering content. Yet he is a hard worker, social, and eager to be part of a typical class. The teachers can see that they will really need to collaborate and plan lessons so that Ramond can learn the material. Although they are worried about the fast pace and scope of their various curriculums, they are up for the new challenges they will face while teaching Ramond. The teachers have learned through their experiences in co-teaching that together they can guide students to learn well beyond original expectations.

———————●◦●———————

Co-teaching is the pairing of a special education teacher and a general education teacher in an inclusive general education classroom for the purpose of providing high-level instruction to meet the diverse needs of a wide range of students. The inclusive classroom has students with and without legally classified disabilities. For example, the short vignette portrays Ramond, a student with significant learning difficulties, who will attend co-taught classes in which co-teachers can address his learning needs.

Co-teaching is not *team teaching*, the practice of two general education teachers combining their classes and teaching some or many lessons. Nor should co-teaching be confused with the practice of adding a paraprofessional to a general education teacher's inclusive classroom.

What led to the co-teaching movement?

The growth in co-teaching can be traced to the changing dimensions of special education in the United States. Until 1975, there was no federal mandate regarding the education of children with disabilities and millions of children were denied an education because educators felt they couldn't meet the needs of students with disabilities. That year, landmark legislation provided the legal basis for educating children with disabilities with the passage of Public Law 94-142, the Education for All Handicapped Children Act. From that historic point on, every school district in the country was mandated to provide a free and appropriate education to all children with disabilities (U.S. Department of Education, 2007).

Under the new federal legislation, students exhibiting difficulties needed to be classified as having a disability and also deemed in need of special education services to qualify for an Individualized Educational Program (IEP) that specified placement, related services, and testing modifications, as well as goals for academic and social improvement.

Despite the good intentions of the 1975 act, many students with special needs remained forever in separate special education placements with social and educational ramifications. Although students with special needs now had access to special education services, many were taught in segregated settings that were not always in their neighborhood schools and had restricted access to typically achieving peers and learning environments. Both social and academic performance gaps (Deshler, n.d.) between students with and without disabilities became apparent, and achievement levels of both groups became increasingly disparate throughout the school years.

A call for reform ensued with the first major effort being the Regular Education Initiative proposed by Madeleine C. Will, former assistant secretary of education (Will, 1986). Will advocated for the merging of special and regular education through what is now known as the Inclusive Movement. Both the Regular Education Initiative and the Inclusive Education Movement expect that many, if not most, students with disabilities will be taught in the general education setting.

Co-teaching, the pairing of general and special educators in a general education classroom, is one of the supportive structures to ensure an appropriate education for a student with disabilities in an inclusive setting. Co-teaching is the most popular inclusive educational model to meet the educational needs of students with disabilities previously enrolled in exclusive, segregated settings (Magiera & Zigmond, 2005).

What services are available to students with special needs?

Children with special needs are taught in a wide variety of settings from the least restrictive (general education class with related services) to the most exclusive (homebound or hospital facility), with integrated co-teaching as part of the continuum. Here is a description of the continuum of services available to students with special needs:

- **General education class,** which includes students who receive the majority of their education program in a typical classroom and receive special education and related services in pull-out sessions.
- **Consultant teacher services,** which provide direct and indirect services to students with special needs who attend regular education classes, including career and technical education classes.
- **Resource room** provided outside the general education classroom for the purpose of providing support and remediation for students with special needs.
- **Integrated co-teaching,** which provides specially designed instruction and academic instruction to a group of students with and without special needs in an inclusive classroom.
- **Separate class,** which includes students who receive special education and related services outside the regular classroom.
- **Separate school,** which includes students who receive special education and related services in separate day schools.
- **Residential facility,** which includes students who receive education in a public or private residential facility, at public expense.
- **Homebound or hospital environment,** which includes students placed in and receiving special education in hospital or homebound programs.

In fall 2007, some 95 percent of 6- to 21-year-old students with special needs were served in neighborhood schools; 3 percent were served in a separate school for students with disabilities; 1 percent were placed in regular private schools by their parents; and less than 1 percent each were served in one of the following environments: in a separate residential facility, homebound or in a hospital, or in a correctional facility (National Center for Education Statistics, 2010).

Why co-teach?

The effective teaching of students with special needs is a major educational and social issue in the United States. The No Child Left Behind (NCLB) legislation clearly targets students who have difficulties learning and the educational systems responsible for growth in learning. Why is this important? As compared with typically achieving students, students with special needs are more likely to be retained for at least one year (26 percent), have a lower graduation rate (41 percent drop out), are less likely to go to college, have less earning potential, and are more likely to be involved in our penal system (Bowe, 2006). The United

States classifies nearly 7 million students, from 3 years old to 21 years old, as being in need of special education services (Aud et al., 2011). The need for an effective education program for these students is clear.

To provide an intensive educational environment for students with significant learning needs, many districts are increasingly opting to institute co-teaching models. Many students who would have been in self-contained special education classes or in special settings are now part of inclusive classrooms— thus, the need for two teachers, one of whom is a special education teacher. As co-teachers, the special education teacher and the general education teacher share the responsibility of educating all students in the class. Together, they understand the needs of each student, plan effective instruction, exchange roles and responsibilities, and employ flexible teaching practices to create opportunities for student learning.

What is the difference between mainstreaming and inclusion?

There is a fundamental difference between mainstreaming and inclusion. Mainstreaming is the practice of integrating students with disabilities into a general education setting, moving them from a special education setting. Mainstreamed students "earn" their way into the general education class by demonstrating academic and behavior levels considered to be within the accepted range of the general education classroom. Mainstreaming puts the onus on the student to make the grade, so to speak, in order to be included in the general education setting. In addition to academic mainstreaming, social mainstreaming is also done in nonacademic classes so that students with special needs in segregated settings can interact with typically achieving peers. Traditionally, students from special education classes are mainstreamed for periods such as lunch, recess, and art.

Inclusion, on the other hand, assumes that the general education setting is the most appropriate setting for most, if not all, students. Students do not have to earn their way into the general education classroom, and supports are put into place to ensure their needs are met. These supports take on a variety of forms (as outlined in the IEP) and may include co-teachers, paraprofessionals, curriculum adaptations, accommodations, test modifications, specifically designed materials, and technology and supportive services from counselors, social workers, and psychologists.

While special education is considered a service and not a place, under the reauthorization of the Individuals with Disabilities Education Improvement Act (IDEIA, 2004), there is a presumption of inclusion in the general education setting for students with disabilities. In other words, school districts are required to ensure that students classified as having disabilities and in need of special education services are given every opportunity to be educated with their typically achieving peer group.

Understanding the differences between mainstreaming and inclusion helps to set the tone of the learning environment. The emphasis on inclusion demands that tasks and professional supports create environments that provide for optimal learning. Professionals in the inclusive co-teaching setting, understanding the diverse and sometimes extensive needs of students, orchestrate learning opportunities for all students. Although an inclusive setting might not be optimal in all circumstances, for the most part, student profiles are looked at to learn not how the student should change but how the environment can support each student's success. Admittedly, just placing students with special needs in a classroom with two teachers does not guarantee success. If students are to be successful, the co-teaching program must have many working components.

What are the goals of co-teaching?

On the most basic level, special education services (wherever they are performed) are aimed at providing a student with disabilities access to an appropriate education and ultimately a high school diploma. Therefore, the goal of co-teaching is to provide an educational environment that emphasizes effective instructional practices through which all students learn and achieve success. Of course, if students with special needs require more intensive instruction, the continuum of services (from an inclusive class to residential facility) is available.

If the inclusive setting with co-teaching is deemed appropriate, the goals for students go far beyond access to a diploma. Academic growth of students is supported as IEP goals are addressed and exposure to rigorous curriculum and higher-order thinking increases. Social growth is also supported with opportunities to interact in a more typical educational setting, thus providing increased opportunities for friendships. The students also benefit from being exposed to two caring adults who can offer assistance, support, expertise, and different points of view.

What are the benefits of co-teaching?

Co-teaching is becoming a popular educational model for addressing inclusion. Although research specifically investigating student outcomes of co-teaching is scarce and somewhat conflicting, many administrators, teachers, parents and students involved in co-teaching give anecdotal evidence of the benefits. Among the benefits described:

• Every student in the class, both typically achieving and those with disabilities, is provided different educational options—from smaller groups and more individualized attention to materials and instruction that take into consideration a wide range of interests and abilities.

• Classroom participation of students with disabilities is increased through the reduction of student-to-teacher ratios and the use of groupings. (These benefits extend to general education students in co-taught classes.)

• Intensity of instruction is achieved through an understanding of student needs, attention to curriculum challenges, use of a variety of effective teaching and learning strategies, adaptation of materials, and continual assessment.

• The stigma often attached to students attending segregated special education classes is reduced.

• Students learn tolerance and respect for diversity.

• Professionals positively support each other's efforts by jointly planning and executing lessons, solving problems, and combining strengths.

• The achievement and social gaps between typically achieving students and students with disabilities are diminished.

• Expectations for students with disabilities are increased.

What are the advantages of being a co-teacher?

Teaching can be an isolating experience, and co-teaching offers professionals the opportunity to collaborate, problem-solve, and create, all in an effort to provide supportive and effective learning for all students. Co-teaching can be fun with increased teacher interchanges providing opportunities for closer interactions with students. Co-teaching is demanding, but sharing responsibilities can create a positive teaching environment.

Administrators and supervisors who acknowledge the multitude of demands inherent in the co-teaching experience can show their support by providing planning time for teachers and relieving co-teachers of certain assignments such as hall duty or giving monetary compensation for after-school planning. Some districts provide opportunities for visiting co-taught classes and professional development workshops. The biggest perk for co-teaching is successful students.

What are some concerns regarding co-teaching?

Alongside the potential benefits of co-teaching are potential obstacles. Any new or unfamiliar practice is usually met with resistance, and co-teaching is not an exception. Researchers, administrators, and co-teachers are sometimes reluctant to endorse or start co-teaching programs because they rely heavily on a positive working relationship between two teachers, require high levels of teaching expertise, demand knowledge of both curriculum and remediation, and require time and effort for adequate planning. Concerns about co-teaching include the following:

- The needs of students with special needs may be put ahead of the needs of typically achieving students.
- Lack of hard data that explores educational outcomes of the students with and without disabilities in co-taught settings.
- Inadequate professional development on information and details unique to co-teaching.
- Slow adoption of new routines that include another equal professional in the classroom, particularly by teachers accustomed to working independently.
- Insufficient time to plan units and lessons.
- Failure of administrators to acknowledge co-teacher preferences to stay together or to separate.
- An inappropriate ratio of students with and without disabilities in a classroom.
- Poor pairing of teachers by administrators.
- Perceived or real hesitation of general education teachers to share the chalk with special education teachers.
- Curriculum and high-stakes testing demands overshadowing the needs of the students with special needs.
- Damage to self-esteem of some students as they struggle with content while others achieve success.

What research supports the effectiveness of co-teaching?

The research on co-teaching can be divided into three phases. The first phase, primarily descriptive, introduced the concept of co-teaching in general education classes and outlined its usefulness as a way of meeting the demands of more students with special needs in the least restrictive setting. Descriptions of various models of co-teaching gave a face to what it could look like in the classroom: one teaching, one supporting; station teaching; parallel teaching; alternative teaching; and teaming (Cook & Friend, 1995; Vaughn, Schumm, Shay, & Arguelles, 1997).

The second phase of research addressed some of the realities of co-teaching and the obstacles to effective co-teaching. Proponents delineated roles and relationships of co-teachers and ways to determine how advanced the co-teaching pairs were in becoming expert co-teachers (Gately & Gately, 2001). Collaboration between the co-teachers was emphasized; and investigations into perceptions of parents, general and special education students, and teachers related to co-teaching generally found positive attitudes while recognizing various roadblocks (Austin, 2001; Tichenor, Heins, & Piechura-Couture, 2000; Wilson & Michaels, 2006). Research analyzing actual co-teacher practices was somewhat critical of the actual use and benefits of two teachers in the classroom (Zigmond, 2001).

The beginning of a third phase of co-teaching research relates to student outcomes, testing the actual effectiveness of co-teaching. Research of educational outcomes of students in co-teaching settings yield somewhat conflicting findings that both question and support the effectiveness of co-teaching for students who have significant learning difficulties (Murawski & Swanson, 2001; Wilson, Kim, & Michaels, 2011). Research on the actual effectiveness of co-teaching is particularly problematic and scarce. Students served in co-taught classes often differ from district to district, and there is no consensus as to what would define effectiveness.

Research on the effectiveness of co-teaching is needed. Ultimately, those involved in co-taught programs must evaluate the effectiveness in their individual settings, based on criteria that they determine to be important.

What are the basic aspects of successful co-teaching?

Successful co-teaching happens when educators, communities, and researchers recognize and support the integral, significant role that co-teaching plays in an inclusive general education classroom marked by diversity at all educational levels, from pre-school through high school. Two of the most important aspects of successful co-teaching:

Strong support from administration. Support is in the form of thoughtfully selecting co-teachers, prioritizing scheduling of co-taught classes, providing training and planning time, and respecting reasonable ratios of students with and without disabilities in the inclusive classroom.

The determination of co-teachers to meet the needs of all students in the classroom. Co-teachers can meet the needs of students by respecting each other's strengths, keeping communication open, identifying the needs of the students, designing curriculum and lessons through which all students can learn, and supporting every student's efforts.

What do co-teaching programs look like at the elementary level?

Elementary co-teaching programs take on various forms, depending on the school and district. Commonly, one general education teacher and one special education teacher are assigned to a class of students. The class includes typically achieving students and students with disabilities. Here are two common elementary level models with their advantages or disadvantages:

Both co-teachers are with the class all day. This model provides opportunity for the co-teachers to collaboratively plan, teach, and reflect, thus eliminating pull-out sessions in which students leave the class throughout the day to receive services, such as speech and language therapy, physical therapy, and occupational therapy. When the co-teachers are together for the entire day, they have more flexibility in scheduling so that student needs and services can be met in the classroom.

The general education teacher is with the class all day, and the special education teacher is assigned some time each day to join the class. With this program model, a teacher assistant typically assists the general education teacher when the special education teacher is not in the room. Although this model might be less costly than a full-time model, establishing parity between the co-teachers is extremely difficult since the special education co-teacher is in the class only part-time. Time restrictions allow for little flexibility; curriculum demands and IEP academic goals can rarely be adequately addressed in this truncated model.

What do co-teaching programs look like at the secondary level?

Secondary programs, like their elementary counterparts, have no single format and reflect district and state policies. Here are some common models:

One general education teacher and one special education teacher are assigned to teach one or more classes together. The general education class includes both typically achieving students and students with disabilities. The co-teachers teach this class period together each day. Or, the special education teacher is in the class every other day (with a teacher assistant in the class on the alternate days).

A special education teacher is assigned a group of students. The special education teacher "follows" a specific group of students with special needs to each content area. The special education teacher in this situation will have to plan with each content teacher (usually social studies, English, math, science).

A special education teacher is given a "specialty" area. The special educator's focus area might be 9th and 10th grade social studies; therefore, he or she co-teaches with one or more 9th and 10th grade general education social studies teachers.

A special education teacher is assigned two specialty areas. For example, the special education teacher's focus area might be math and science or social studies and English on one grade level. In this arrangement, the special education teacher co-teaches the math and science classes with multiple content teachers.

A special education teacher is assigned a support class. In addition to the co-taught sessions, the special education teacher typically has a separate period each day to work with the students with disabilities on IEP and general education curriculum goals.

How many students are usually in a co-taught class?

Class size varies according to district or state policies. In inclusive classrooms, the ratio of students with disabilities to typically achieving students becomes important. In some classrooms, students with disabilities make up anywhere from 10 to 50 percent of the total population.

A high percentage of students with disabilities in a class is problematic, as it reduces the positive effects of groupings and interactions with typically achieving peers. Some districts have tried to address this problem by increasing class size so that the ratio is more proportional. Theoretically, even the larger class size can be justified because of the benefits of the co-teaching model. Some districts have opted to keep the total class size small, limiting the number of students with disabilities in the class and using the special education teacher only on alternate days.

The matter of class size and proportion is critical, and administrators and teachers should be vigilant in monitoring the effect of the ratio on the success of students in the co-taught inclusive class. An overrepresentation of students with disabilities in a single class does not meet the spirit of inclusion and needs to be avoided. While a hard and fast percentage is difficult to ascertain, 30 percent of students with disabilities in one class is probably the upper limit for a program that aims to be effective.

Should there be paraprofessionals in a co-taught class?

Students with disabilities in inclusive classrooms may have disabilities that substantially affect learning, so often other support staff are assigned to assist the students and the co-teachers. Some students with disabilities will require a dedicated aide mandated by the IEP. Some districts routinely put a paraprofessional in co-taught classes.

Teacher assistants, aides, and paraprofessionals can offer invaluable services in a co-taught class, and the co-teachers and administrators need to support and nurture their efforts. Although it might seem that the more adults in a classroom the better, there are instances when there are many more adults than are needed. In addition, teacher assistants, aides, and paraprofessionals are often not given training in co-teaching and might not be properly directed by the co-teachers. See Chapter 9 for more information on paraprofessionals.

What is the relationship between co-taught settings and Response to Intervention practices?

In efforts to decrease the referrals to special education and to meet the needs of students having learning difficulties in general education settings, many districts are designing Response to Intervention (RtI) systems. RtI usually consists of tiers of instructional practices beginning at the classroom level and then offering layers of increasingly more intense instruction and remediation. Although the design and implementation of RtI varies, most include high-quality instruction using research-based and evidenced-based instructional methods and programs, and ongoing progress monitoring. Murawski and Hughes (2009) contend that co-taught settings can uniquely meet the goals of RtI because through co-teaching "lessons are research based... address the wide variety of needs in the general education classroom... ensure access to the general education curriculum for diverse learners... [use] ongoing data collection and progress monitoring.... and students... are able to receive specialized and more individualized instruction in small groups" (p. 269).

Case Study 1

How can we address some of the unanticipated consequences of a successful co-taught inclusion setting?

Ms. Munion and Mr. Felps, co-teachers, have successfully worked together for the past three years. They regularly plan together, employ great teaching strategies, and students are successful. The district initially set the proportion of students with special needs to no more than 30 percent. However, the co-teachers' reputations are spreading, and many parents of students who are not classified but have some learning and attention difficulties are requesting this co-taught class. At this point, there are more students with some needs in the class than students without.

Statement of the problem

Loading a class with atypical students may sabotage the potential benefits of a heterogeneous inclusive class.

Problem genesis

The individualization and effective instruction that these co-teachers established are difficult to replicate in a solo-taught class, and parents of students who can use some extra attention are seeking the co-taught class.

How the problem is being denied or addressed

The co-taught class is becoming a class for students with special needs. While unclassified students with particular needs can benefit from a co-taught class, there should be a concerted effort to keep the co-taught class as heterogeneous as possible. There needs to be a mix of all levels of achievement in the class so that expectations and levels of interaction remain high.

How to promote a positive outcome

• These co-teachers obviously achieved a high degree of expertise and effectiveness. Many of the strategies that they use may be beneficial for a solo-taught class. They can share their methods with other teachers by establishing collegial circles or professional development workshops, or by sharing materials.

• Principals, guidance counselors, and teachers are usually responsible for finalizing the makeup of classes. Considerable effort needs to be exerted to keep co-taught classes as heterogeneous as possible. If there are many at-risk students at a particular grade level, rather than assigning most of them to the co-taught class (as in this example), the principal may disperse them throughout the other sections of the grade, provide a teacher aide, or have services such as speech and reading pushed into the solo-taught classes.

———————— •◦• ————————

Case Study 2

How can we address the needs of low-performing students in a co-taught class?

Ms. Kenyen, a special education teacher, and Mr. Benson, a general education teacher, co-teach a 9th grade Intermediate Algebra class. Both teachers are certified in math and are confident with the curriculum. Mr. Benson has been teaching for 15 years and developed a teaching regimen that incorporates many learning strategies helpful to students experiencing math difficulties: all papers given to students are numbered and have holes punched; notes are given in a guided note format; each lesson contains a review of previous material, a scaffolded lesson, and guided practice. During a typical class period, the co-teachers do variations of team teaching and one teach, one support. Their roles fluctuate, and there is obvious parity between the teachers and in the eyes of the students. The class is relatively large, consisting of 28 students. Fourteen of the students have identified specific learning difficulties ranging from learning disabilities in math to autism. Many of the students in the class have focusing, organizational, and behavioral difficulties. The co-teachers are happy with how they are working together but are concerned because the majority of the students are not performing well on tests.

Statement of the problem

Despite a strongly developed curriculum, additional math support classes, a wonderful co-teaching relationship between the teachers, and good rapport among the teachers and students, students are not performing adequately.

Problem genesis

Math can be a particularly difficult subject for students with special needs. The pacing is often quick, leaving little time to develop skills. Skills and topics build on one another, so not doing well on one topic often has dire consequences for the next topic.

How the problem is being denied or addressed

The students with special needs are supported through a daily small-group support class taught by the special education co-teacher. They are further supported by a math lab held every other day, which is also available to all students. In math lab, a different general education math teacher reinforces the math skills as he or she pre-teaches and post-teaches the general education class curriculum.

How to promote a positive outcome

• The students have a tremendous amount of support available to them. The question arises as to how the support is integrated and coordinated. The teacher of the math lab class needs to clearly understand where a particular student's skills break down on specific topics and to offer targeted and intensive teaching on the topics and skills needed for proficiency.

• The co-teachers work wonderfully together, and the class content is well defined and executed. However, despite the various roles that the co-teachers play, they do not take advantage of the opportunity to use powerful co-teaching approaches, such as parallel teach (Chapter 2), and thus to provide more intensive and individualized instruction. The co-teachers should try parallel teaching, perhaps starting with two groups to review for quizzes and tests. After that, the co-teachers might progress to having two groups for start-of-class Do Now assignments and guided practices; eventually they may each teach the material.

It took a while for us to embrace parallel teaching. Our classroom is really small and oddly shaped and we can barely fit desks for all the students and there is little room to move around. We thought that we and the students would get distracted but we knew it was a good idea and we kept trying. Now we parallel teach all the time and know that students are learning and participating.

—*General education high school co-teacher*

We most often use one teach, one support. Sometimes we do teaming but it usually happens naturally rather than planned, when we add or help each other out. We can do that because we've been together for such a long time.

—*Special education high school co-teacher*

At first we always put students into small groups and we would both walk around and supervise. Now that each of us (teachers) is directly teaching a station, we're finding that students are really learning more.

—*General education 6th grade co-teacher*

When I go into a co-taught class I want to see both teachers teaching and interacting with students.

—*High school assistant principal*

2

Delving into the Details

Ms. Jonas is so excited. She finally convinced Ms. Brickstone to divide the class into two groups to discuss *House on Mango Street*. In a class of 30 students, 7 have significant reading and writing difficulties and 4 have attention problems. Both teachers are enjoying their first year co-teaching together. Ms. Brickstone always tells great stories and has a wonderful way of guiding discussion. Ms. Jonas knows Ms. Brickstone likes to run the discussion with the entire class, but both teachers have observed that most of the students with learning difficulties rarely participate. Ms. Jonas is not sure that the students are following the discussion. She knows it would be better to split the class in half so that more students participate in the discussion and so that each teacher can better assess learning. Although it's taken half of the year for Ms. Brickstone to agree to use two discussion groups, Ms. Jonas has high hopes that the parallel discussions will be successful and Ms. Brickstone will want to do more teaching in groups.

Ms. Brickstone sits with a group of 15 students and starts a discussion on the *House on Mango Street*. She loves this book and so do the students. As her group discusses the chapter, she hears Ms. Jonas discussing the same chapter with her group of 15 students. Ms. Brickstone is trying to concentrate on her own group, but she keeps listening to hear if Ms. Jonas is hitting the important points. Ms. Brickstone knows that by breaking the class into two groups, she and Ms. Jonas will double the amount of student responses, and it will be easier to see if instruction needs to be customized. Today it took a long time to get the students into their groups, and the small room dictates little distance separating the two groups. Ms. Brickstone also knows that this is the first time Ms. Jonas has taught using this book. Ms. Brickstone has used the book for five years and understands the symbolism and narrations and worries that the students in Ms. Jonas's group won't get a deep understanding of the book. Ms. Brickstone takes a deep breath as she realizes that it's going to take time to learn how to effectively teach two groups and to trust Ms. Jonas's abilities. She is willing to give it a try. Ms. Brickstone also knows that some students don't pay attention when she teaches to the whole class and hopes that with some practice she and Ms. Jonas will iron out the difficulties.

What are the various co-teaching approaches or models?

The most popular approaches or most frequently used models of co-teaching include one teach, one support; parallel teaching; station teaching; alternative teaching; and teaming. Refer to Figure 2.1 for a visual explanation of how classrooms are typically set up if a co-teaching team wants to arrange the classroom to facilitate a certain co-teaching model.

One Teach, One Support

One teacher (Teacher A) has primary responsibility for teaching the content material to the entire class while the other teacher (Teacher B) observes students, circulates through the room giving students support and assistance as needed, and interjects general comments and suggestions to the class. In the best co-teaching situations, each teacher frequently serves each role (primary or support) depending on the lesson. See Figure 2.1 for a typical classroom arrangement.

The positive aspects of the one teach, one support model:

Figure 2.1 | Classroom Configurations for Co-Teaching Classrooms

One Teach, One Support

Teacher A instructs whole class

Teacher B supports

Parallel Teaching

Teacher A

Teacher B

*Students face their
group's teacher*

Station Teaching

3 Stations

Teacher A   Teacher B

Independent

4 Stations

Teacher A   Independent

Independent   Teacher B

Alternative Teaching

Teacher A   Teacher B

Figure 2.1 | Classroom Configurations for Co-Teaching Classrooms—(continued)

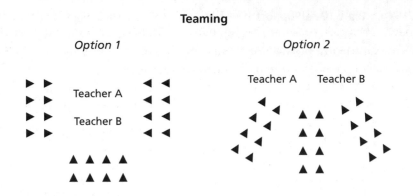

- Many students in the class can receive individual attention.
- Students are given gentle reminders to stay on task.
- Student confusion can be individually resolved.
- Informal assessment of student learning occurs easily and naturally.
- Little planning time is needed.

The challenging aspects of this model:

- Parity can be severely compromised when one teacher assumes a dominant position and students perceive teachers as unequal.
- The supporting teacher may be perceived as an aide and not a teacher.
- The supporting teacher may feel that he or she is not sufficiently contributing to the instruction of students.
- Students do not get the intensity of instruction needed.

The best time to use the one teach, one support model:

- When planning time is very limited.
- When whole group instruction seems most appropriate.
- When co-teachers are beginning to become adjusted to each other's styles.
- When the special educator is learning the content.

Special considerations related to using this co-teaching model: One teach, one support is the most frequently used model in co-taught classes. While co-teachers defend this model stating that the assessment and individual support that is given to students more than justifies it, the one teach, one support approach does not provide the intensity of instruction and support that co-teachers can ideally provide. If this is the default model used by co-teachers, they are seriously neglecting more powerful models.

Parallel Teaching

The class is divided into two heterogeneous groups. Each teacher directly instructs the same content to half the group. See Figure 2.1 for a typical classroom arrangement.

The positive aspects of using parallel teaching:

- Immediately decreases the student-to-teacher ratio by half.
- Increases possibility of more students responding and participating in class discussions.
- Increases teachers' abilities to access student understanding.
- Parity of teachers is possible.

The challenging aspects of this model:

- Thorough planning is necessary.
- Both teachers must have mastery of content.
- The teachers must carefully synchronize time.
- Some teachers and students have difficulty adjusting to multiple people speaking at the same time (although many report that, with practice, this is not a detracting factor).
- Some classrooms are not physically conducive to this model.

Parallel teaching is a particularly effective model to use when the teachers are equally confident with the content. It may be used to introduce new content but can also be used to create a more intensive environment for test review, a review of test answers, homework review, and guided practice.

Special considerations related to using this co-teaching model: Many co-teachers seem to understand the benefits of this model but feel that it is too distracting for both teachers and students. With some time and practice, teachers and students learn to ignore distractions and appreciate the intensity of instruction afforded by this approach. Care must be taken in positioning the groups and teachers to minimize distractions and optimize instruction. The co-teachers should face each other on opposite sides of the room. Students in group 1 face Teacher A; students in group 2 face Teacher B. The students are then not distracted as they would be if they were facing each other.

Station Teaching

This co-teaching approach divides the class into two, three, or four heterogeneous groups. Each teacher directly instructs a group on a particular aspect of the topic while students in other groups work independently on materials that reinforce or extend their skills. After an appropriate, allotted amount of time has elapsed, the groups (or teachers) rotate.

The positive aspects of using station teaching:

- Teacher parity is highlighted.
- Student-to-teacher ratio decreases.
- Student response rate is increased.
- Differentiated instruction is possible.
- Personal attention and assessment are improved.

The challenging aspects of using this model:

- Precise planning of content and groupings are necessary.
- Students must be able to work cooperatively or independently if there are three or more groups.
- Noise level in the classroom may increase.

Station teaching is useful when particular skills need to be developed in small, concentrated, and focused lessons. For instance, when working on a unit related to the figures of speech, one teacher might focus on similes, the other teaches on metaphors, while the independent group engages in a creative writing assignment. Groups then rotate so all students participate in each station.

Special considerations related to using this model of co-teaching is that particular attention must be taken while setting up the groups. There may be a tendency to group students according to ability level. Although grouping by ability may be appropriate at times, the goal is heterogeneous groupings in which students' memberships are often switched. With frequent use, students easily go into assigned groups with little class disturbance.

Alternative Teaching

In the alternative teaching model, one teacher is responsible for the large group of students while the other teacher instructs a small group of students.

The positive aspects of using alternative teaching:

• Provides a unique opportunity to deliver intensive and individualized instruction to students.

• Offers opportunities for reinforcement or enrichment to a smaller group of students.

The challenging aspects of using this model:

• Overuse can lead to segregated practices within the class.

• If teachers occasionally take the smaller group to another room because of noise or space considerations, care must be taken to avoid any negative consequences and potential stigma attributed to those students.

Alternative teaching can be used any time there is a need for small group instruction. One creative use of alternative teaching is to have the larger group work on an activity with supervision from one co-teacher, while the other co-teacher meets with three students to discuss their academic progress, specific questions about the work, and address their questions. Remember to rotate membership in the small groups and to ensure that each student meets with a teacher regularly.

Alternative teaching allows for the much-needed opportunity to work in a small intensive setting, but group membership must be rotated to avoid stigma that may be attributed to certain small groups of students going to the "back table."

Teaming

In this co-teaching model, both teachers teach and support each other and the students at the same time. Both teachers are adept at curriculum content and effective teaching and learning techniques and have established professional equity and parity. Teaming doesn't look like a game of tag with each teacher taking turns at teaching. The co-teachers, teaching to the entire class, contribute equally and importantly to the lesson by taking particular sides, demonstrating different ways of thinking or approaching a task, or highlighting important elements. They both attend to the learning needs of the students and are able to adjust and adapt their teaching as the need arises. For instance, the co-teachers can plan to teach a lesson to the entire class and then, as the lesson progresses, decide to quickly go into two groups to target obvious gaps in student understanding.

The positive aspects of teaming:

- Creates a highly dynamic classroom.
- Supports parity of teachers because they run the classroom collaboratively.
- Allows presentation of information in multiple ways with multiple perspectives.
- Promotes respect between teachers as they also serve as a model for students respecting one another.
- Facilitates flexible groupings, as needed.

The challenging aspects of this model:

- Masquerades as one teach, one support if one teacher simply offers comments or perspectives during a class. Teaming is interactive and intensive.
- Requires a high degree of expertise in both content and process from both teachers.

The best time to use this model is when the presentation of differing views and perspective is appropriate.

Teaming is generally done during whole-group instruction. Co-teachers need to make sure that they are intensifying instruction and have the flexibility to go into smaller groupings when more focused instruction is appropriate. Co-teachers may be tag-team teaching (each takes a turn presenting the material) instead of teaming.

Are both co-teachers responsible for all students?

Of course! One of the greatest benefits of co-teaching is that all students in the classroom receive more support. When special education services were relegated to specific places like a resource room, students who were not classified as having disabilities were left without extra help in general education settings. Students who had some difficulties and were struggling, but did not qualify for specific special education services, received little special support. In the co-taught class, the focus on how materials are constructed, how content is presented, how assignments and exams are created, and how students are supported can benefit all students.

In a co-taught class, is it OK if the special education teacher walks around and helps students instead of teaching?

The issue isn't if it is OK to walk around; the question is if there is a more effective use of teacher time. Is one teacher walking around and helping students because the co-teachers did not plan? Or do they feel that this is the best approach to optimize student learning on this particular task? If the answer is that this is the best model for this task at this time, then it is appropriate to work the room and help students. If the approach is chosen because of lack of planning, it is important for the co-teachers to seriously reconsider their routines.

Co-teachers who use a variety of co-teaching approaches and use smaller groupings (such as parallel and stations in their classrooms) can see the benefits to students. These co-teachers can better differentiate instruction, assess understanding, increase participation, decrease behavior problems, and focus attention than a single teacher working with an entire classroom.

When are the students with special needs pulled out for intensive instruction?

There really shouldn't be unbreakable rules in co-teaching. Co-teachers need to discuss the rationale for everything that is done in the co-taught inclusion class and choose the appropriate approach by asking themselves: Why are students being pulled out? Which students are being pulled out? How often are students pulled out? Which co-teacher is doing the pull-out instruction? Are students being stigmatized? And, most important, could the same instruction be done within the classroom?

Occasionally, special education teachers who are accustomed to more segregated settings think that the only way to offer intensive instruction is in a location separate from the classroom. If co-teachers brainstorm ways instruction can be intensified within the class (for instance, with station teaching), they often come up with in-class solutions that meet the needs of the students. Co-teaching is an inclusive practice. Segregating students defeats the intent.

What about the noise level in the classroom when teachers are co-teaching?

It's interesting that co-teachers can usually deal with the noise level of cooperative groups in a class but anticipate noise issues with parallel teaching and station teaching. Teachers do need to modulate the volume of their voices when simultaneously teaching groups, but most learn the art with experience. Students usually quickly adjust. Co-teachers should experiment and reflect on what worked and what was distracting. Then they can consider ways to see how the noise can be less distracting. The co-teaching experience is most effective when teachers create frequent opportunities for small-group, directly taught instruction.

How do you deal with classrooms that are just too small?

The reality is that many classrooms are small, and this is a particular challenge when co-teachers need to teach in parallel groups or stations. Grouping students with just chairs instead of chairs and desks, or having students sit on the floor in groups on different sides of the room often helps. Again, the co-teachers can experiment to try to make the best of the difficult situation. Administration can also anticipate the need for adequate classroom space by assigning larger classrooms to co-taught inclusive classes.

———◦•◦———

Case Study 3

How can we change the reliance on the one teach, one support model of co-teaching?

Ms. Perman is a general education teacher and has taught 9th grade math for 10 years. Mr. Ernest has been a special education resource room teacher for 4 years. Ms. Perman and Mr. Ernest are co-teaching for the first time. Ms. Perman teaches the class and Mr. Ernest walks around the room to make sure that students understand assignments and are on-task. Mr. Ernest answers questions and intervenes whenever a behavior issue becomes apparent. Mr. Ernest and Ms. Perman have one period every other day that is reserved for co-planning; however, Ms. Perman always plans the lessons and lets Mr. Ernest know what general topics will be covered. Mr. Ernest usually uses the planning time to photocopy materials that Ms. Perman has made for the class. Ms. Perman and Mr. Ernest like their arrangement and camaraderie.

Statement of the problem

Ms. Perman and Mr. Ernest rely on the easiest but perhaps the least effective model of co-teaching, which is one teach, one support. The models of co-teaching that divide classes into smaller groupings, such as stations and parallel teaching, enable co-teachers to increase participation, sustain student attention, and intensify instruction.

Problem genesis

Ms. Perman and Mr. Ernest are not co-planning. Without co-planning, the one teach, one support model is often the default since no specialized roles are predetermined.

How the problem is being denied or addressed

Mr. Ernest and Ms. Perman seem happy with the relationship and the way they co-teach. Their reliance on one model of co-teaching, however, reduces the potential student learning that could be afforded by having two teachers in a classroom. The administration doesn't seem to offer guidance on how to co-teach.

Ways of promoting a positive outcome

• Using the scheduled planning period every other day to plan collaboratively would reap major benefits. When two teachers co-plan, they have the opportunity to make adjustments to content, presentation, and materials.

• While planning together, Mr. Ernest and Ms. Perman should make an effort to mix up their co-teaching by using at least two different co-teaching approaches during each teaching period. By extending their comfort zone, Ms.

Perman and Mr. Ernest might see the benefits of parallel teaching, station teaching, or alternative teaching.

• Visiting other co-teaching classes or watching co-teaching videos to observe how others approach co-teaching could help these co-teachers envision different models and how they can actually work.

• Instituting co-teaching routines, such as using parallel teaching for test review or teaming for class discussions might be useful.

• Committing to planning and incorporating other co-teaching models in their classroom, Ms. Perman and Mr. Ernest will find student learning maximized.

———————— •●• ————————

Case Study 4

How can we change a situation where two teachers do not know how to co-teach?

Mr. Masone and Ms. Pelizzi are assigned to co-teach a 9th grade English class. Although each teacher has 20 years' of experience, they have never co-taught classes, nor have they received training in co-teaching. When Mr. Masone, the general education teacher, teaches the class, Ms. Pelizzi reformats and adapts exams or calls parents. When Ms. Pelizzi teaches, Mr. Masone visits the guidance counselor to review IEPs. The teachers are seldom in class at the same time, but they feel competent in their own and each other's teaching abilities. Mr. Masone and Ms. Pelizzi are hard workers and love the way they have interpreted co-teaching because they think they are addressing the needs of students with competent teaching, and they feel the flexibility of being co-teachers allows them time to adapt materials, contact parents, and review IEPs.

Statement of the problem

Mr. Masone and Ms. Pelizzi interpret co-teaching as co-caring. They spend their co-teaching time taking turns to indirectly address student needs by using the time to phone parents and create materials.

Problem genesis

The problem can be identified as a lack of training in effective co-teaching, along with little direction and few expectations from the administration.

How the problem is being denied or addressed

The administration appears to have a hands-off policy on co-teaching. And, the teachers do not perceive a problem with their strategy and like their interpretation of co-teaching.

Ways of promoting a positive outcome

• The district must present a clear picture of expectations regarding the co-teaching program. Although common, it is still surprising that a district would invest in co-teaching and not communicate to teachers how to implement the program. A written district statement describing co-teaching could go a long way toward setting a standard.

• Assigning and using a common planning time could help the co-teachers reflect on the needs of students and plan lessons that include using the various models of co-teaching.

• Mr. Masone and Ms. Pelizzi need some instruction regarding co-teaching, specifically about approaches to co-teaching. They could attend regional workshops on co-teaching, consult with co-teaching experts, visit other co-taught classes, or watch videos on co-teaching to gain a needed understanding of effective programs.

• Ms. Pelizzi and Mr. Masone have many of the important components that lead to successful co-teaching, including a professional respect for each other. They should do well with some clear expectations and with some knowledge regarding co-teaching.

I know how important it is to match teachers who will get along with each other and I try my best to make good matches. Most times it works, sometimes it doesn't.

—Middle school administrator

I have a lot of confidence in myself as a teacher but am very apprehensive about embarking on co-teaching. My nightmare is that we are going to spend an entire year not getting along. Our principal paired us, but I'm not sure she put much thought into it. I absolutely love teaching and will be devastated if the whole year becomes a disaster.

—Secondary general education teacher before the start of co-teaching

Co-teaching has been the best teaching experience of my life. I know we don't do everything perfectly or by the book, but we respect each other's views and can get so much more done when we are together. I've learned a great deal from my partner and I am definitely a much better teacher. I don't know if I could ever go back to teaching by myself in a room.

—Elementary general education co-teacher

We've been together for 6 years and I am hoping that we can stay together forever. When something works it shouldn't be messed with.

—Elementary special education co-teacher

3

Establishing and Maintaining Effective Co-Teaching Relationships

Ms. Malone smiles and enters her 3rd grade classroom. She's been co-teaching with Ms. Janson for two months and can't believe the improvement over last year. Memories of feeling like an aide rather than a special education teacher flood her mind. No matter what she did last year, her co-teacher seemed to be annoyed. As time went on, Ms. Malone stopped trying to do the job she was hired to do and did little more than walk around the class and refocus students' attention. Fortunately she saw the students who were classified for an additional period each day, and felt that it made some positive difference in their learning. This year, thankfully, is totally different. Each day, Ms. Malone and Ms. Janson spend time planning. Ms. Janson respects Ms. Malone's opinions and expertise, and together they have a great time teaching in the classroom. Ms. Malone has never worked so hard but feels rejuvenated, effective, and thankful.

Dr. Humphrey walks into the 3rd grade class, not knowing what to expect. Last year Ms. Malone and her co-teacher had a hard time working together; despite monthly visits, Dr. Humphrey saw little change in the co-teachers' behaviors. Although the general education teacher was considered one of the most talented in the school, she taught the class as if she were by herself. Dr. Humphrey couldn't gauge Ms. Malone's competence because she played such a minor role in the class. He hopes that this year, paired with a different general education teacher, Ms. Malone and her new co-teacher will be more collaborative and effective.

How are teachers chosen to work together as co-teachers?

With whom and how teachers are paired to co-teach is fundamental to the success of co-teaching. As depicted in the scenario with Ms. Malone, the same teacher, paired with a different general education teacher is competent and effective. Care must be taken in choosing pairs.

Volunteer

Conventional wisdom says that the two teachers should volunteer to work together. If two teachers voluntarily go into the classroom, most people expect that they have jumped the first and biggest hurdle of co-teaching: teacher compatibility. It is assumed that they like and respect each other, and share common principles and beliefs. Whenever possible, a voluntary system is preferable to teachers being drafted into co-teaching. However, it is a mistake to think just because teachers volunteer that difficulties or differences might not occur. In fact, there are instances where co-teaching has come between friendships, and the co-teachers are bewildered when the experience doesn't work as smoothly as expected.

An interesting situation arises when teachers volunteer to co-teach, but the administrator does not think they are suited for the program. Does the principal honor the volunteers or pick other teachers, knowing the mindset of a volunteer is different from an assigned participant? Both decisions rest on the unknown, and the administrator will be needed to support the pair throughout the year.

Assigned by personality or expertise

Co-teachers are often assigned to teach together by administrators who think they would be a good match. The match might be made based on personalities or expertise, but compatibility is not a given, and care must be taken to support a newly formed co-teacher pair.

Assigned for convenience

Sometimes co-teachers are thrown together by convenience. This most frequently occurs after all other class assignments have been established and there is an unexpected opening in a co-taught class. Just as having teachers volunteer isn't necessarily a formula for success, a makeshift partnership isn't necessarily a formula for failure. Chances for good pairings increase when the partnerships are planned.

Assigned for experience

It is true that a first-year teacher (whether special or general education) faces many new situations and issues. And, figuring things out in full view of a more or less judgmental colleague may add a fair degree of anxiety to the relationship. If the co-teaching partnership works, however, the novice teacher has a tremendous opportunity to learn with and from a more experienced colleague and may avoid some typical first-year hardships. Partnering a veteran and novice teacher can be particularly helpful for pacing issues, gaining understanding of the essential components of the curriculum, and learning from tried and true experiences.

Of course, problems may arise if the partnership doesn't work well and the novice teacher feels intimidated by the veteran teacher. In addition, it may take time for the novice teacher to establish an equal partnership with the more experienced teacher. And, certainly there are instances in which parity is not established and the veteran teacher assumes the major role throughout the year. That sort of co-teaching partnership is not successful and thwarts the growth and development of the new teacher.

If both teachers are beginning teachers and they have mutual respect for the other person's knowledge and work ethic, the excitement of going through their first year together can be positive. Each lesson is new, and the co-teaching pair has the opportunity to develop instruction and materials geared to the diversity of needs in an inclusive setting.

Assigned by master schedule

In many cases, particularly at the secondary level, co-teachers are paired by the master schedule. Unless the co-taught inclusion classes are factored in first, the schedule dictates who teaches classes together. Using the schedule as a default often leads to special education teachers paired with multiple general education teachers and subjects, resulting in inefficient practices.

Assigned by availability

Limited personnel can also dictate who teaches together. In primary and elementary schools, where teachers generally teach the same grade level for many years (and there are only a few special educators), choices for creating optimum partnerships are curtailed.

No matter what the criteria for the pairing—volunteer, friendship, expertise, experience, luck of the draw—addressing the realities of co-teaching partnerships is imperative. Administratively, some things can be done to assist and support positive and successful partnerships. Ultimately, it is the responsibility of the two teachers to join together to make the relationship work for the benefit of the students.

How long should co-teachers stay together?

There is no magical length of time that co-teachers should stay together. The simple answer is long enough for the partners to understand how to deliver high-quality instruction to all students but not so long as the pair becomes complacent. If the partnership is not working, a year is too long. If the co-teachers inspire each other and continue to provide opportunities for learning, then there is no limit on how long they should be kept together. What is known is that co-teachers who develop a good relationship should spend several years together. Co-teaching is a process, and veteran co-teachers often can attain a higher level of effectiveness than new co-teacher pairs. All too often co-teaching partners are separated, only to have to start the process again with another teacher and another curriculum. Frequent changes inhibit co-teachers from becoming proficient in both content and process, particularly at the secondary level.

Despite that advice and the fact that change can be difficult, in some circumstances it is advisable to break up an effective team so that other teachers can benefit from their expertise. And, in other instances, a special education teacher may loop into the next grade with a particular student or group of students to allow for continuity and a potentially smoother and faster transition into the next grade.

Unfortunately, even when there is acknowledgment that effective co-teaching teams should be maintained, tough scheduling decisions often necessitate splitting teams. In time, teachers can adjust, but the transition is smoother when administrators offer the rationale for the change. Administrators who don't make the effort to keep effective teams together do little to support a successful program.

How are positive co-teaching relationships supported?

Effective co-teachers communicate honestly with each other. Honest communication is no easy task, but there are various direct and indirect ways that can help preserve (or create) compatibility. Addressing the needs and challenges of a co-teaching partnership is essential for successful co-teaching.

Open discussions

We've found that newly formed co-teaching teams often shy away from frank discussions regarding their knowledge and understanding of co-teaching, their relationship, classroom procedures, as well as the basics of teaching and learning practices. A framework for talking through the components of a co-teaching experience can be helpful throughout the year but is particularly valuable at the beginning of the school year. While there are checklists and questions for co-teachers (Murawski & Dieker, 2004; Walther-Thomas & Bryant, 1996) the answers to two simple questions can be particularly revealing and form the basis for frank conversations: (1) What is your co-teaching dream? (2) What is your co-teaching nightmare? The answers from co-teachers disclose issues related to control, fairness, competence, work ethic, classroom management, expectations, and what comprises success and failure. The co-teachers thus begin their work together understanding what is most important to each of them. They can then get into the nitty-gritty aspects of co-teaching that must be addressed and discussed. Co-teachers must ask themselves and each other questions about the issues revealed through their disclosure and discussion of dreams and nightmares.

In practice. A co-teaching pair's answers to their co-teaching dream showed that both were passionate and adamant that all students learn and succeed in the inclusive classroom. Their nightmares, however, were quite different. The general education co-teacher feared that the typically achieving students were going to get shortchanged and that she also was not knowledgeable enough to teach students with special needs. The special education co-teacher feared that she was not going to have an equal or respected role and not be able to handle both curriculum and IEP goals. The subsequent conversations centered on how parity of roles could be established and how the co-teachers were going to plan lessons that address the needs and strengths of students of all levels. The co-teachers looked at the different models of co-teaching and decided when each model would be appropriate. They started the year incorporating methods that addressed the needs of the diversity of learners in their classroom.

Alternatively, a series of co-teacher meetings set up by the co-teachers or the administration can serve as a forum to discuss co-teaching issues. These meetings should be scheduled throughout the year with time for specific co-teaching topics as well as spontaneous discussion of challenges as they arise.

Professional learning communities

Professional learning communities are small groups of teachers that meet on a regular basis to learn, discuss, and problem-solve educational issues. In these small groups, teachers break through the often isolating aspects of teaching and set up discovery and learning experiences for the group. Simple steps for setting up a collegial group include (1) forming a small group, (2) focusing on goals, (3) brainstorming a focus, (4) drawing conclusions, (5) planning actions, (6) reflecting, and (7) celebrating (adapted from Siebold, 2008). As part of a professional learning community, co-teachers can visit their colleagues' classes to observe techniques and then meet to discuss aspects of the lesson and co-teaching models used.

In practice. An elementary school with five sets of co-teachers decided to form a discussion group. Each month they read and discussed an article on co-teaching and also discussed issues that arose during their own co-teaching. One excellent by-product of the meetings was the discussions across grade levels where the co-teachers reflected on the type and amount of support and the progress of the students in relation to their various grades.

Discussions with colleagues

Discussion sessions meant for co-teachers to explore their relationship benefit everyone best if a neutral person, such as the school psychologist or counselor, is invited and is allowed to provide perspective. Support personnel have a unique opportunity to provide support to co-teachers in a safe environment.

Unlike direct administration support, where co-teachers may perceive the support as judgmental, the psychologist or counselor can listen to their colleagues, make suggestions, and facilitate communication between the co-teachers in a collegial way.

In practice. An elementary school psychologist took an active role in reviewing the progress of students in the co-taught classes. She routinely observed student performance and discussed the students with their co-teachers. One co-teaching pair, wrestling with personality clashes, met with the psychologist jointly and individually throughout the school year. The psychologist's commitment and involvement mitigated and diffused what might have become explosive situations.

Meetings with administrators

Administrators who understand the complexities of co-teaching can directly support co-teaching partnerships and practices.

In practice. The co-teaching teams in 4th and 5th grade seemed to be constantly changing (even during the school year) because of family emergencies, attrition, and personal leave. In addition, many of the co-teachers within existing pairs had different ideas regarding the level and type of support that students needed and their partner's level of participation and expertise. The principal, realizing that co-taught classes were an important service to students, began to meet bimonthly with each co-teaching team to establish procedures for planning and teaching and to gently guide the co-teachers into more harmonious and effective practices. This principal valued co-teaching and demonstrated this commitment with her time and expertise. As the year went on, the assistant principal assumed the supportive role.

Collaborative problem solving

Focusing on a pressing difficulty can galvanize co-teachers into action and offer the opportunity to look deeply into a problem and find solutions in tandem. Throughout this book we've offered case studies using vignettes of typical co-teaching encounters along with a systemic problem-solving method that addresses the difficulties portrayed. We've modeled the collaborative problem-solving steps to help you apply them to your own situation. The steps are straightforward, yet complex, and use of the Problem-Solving Organizer (Figure 3.1) can guide the process:

1. Vignette: a description of a common co-teaching problem, written in the third person with fictitious characters.

2. Statement of the problem: a simple, one- or two-sentence description of the difficulty. It's important to get to the heart of the problem and state it clearly because a problem cannot be solved until it is plainly defined.

3. Problem genesis: a hard look at what led up to the difficulty. It takes time to generate a one- or two-sentence statement that defines the antecedents of any problem. Knowing what generated the problem gives good insight into how the problem can be solved.

4. How the problem is being denied or addressed: By discussing how the problem is being denied or addressed, the participants can see how the problem is perpetuated.

5. Ways of promoting a positive outcome: Participants brainstorm a series of possible solutions. In most cases, a combination of changes will be required to adequately solve the problem.

Figure 3.1 | The Problem-Solving Organizer

Vignette:		
Statement of the problem:	Problem genesis:	How the problem is being denied or addressed:
Ways of promoting a positive outcome:		

Co-teaching teams, collegial communities, and co-teachers with administrators can collaboratively solve difficulties using the process. Although addressing difficulties head-on can lead to a high degree of defensiveness, blame, and hard feelings, the vignettes supplied allow discussants to depersonalize the situation and look objectively at the issue. When those involved with co-teaching routinely look at common challenges through a nonjudgmental process, they begin to see their own challenges from a different perspective.

Focus on students

When co-teachers focus attention on students and their needs, they begin forming a partnership with a common purpose. Using the table in Figure 3.2 as a guide, co-teachers can look deeply into student behavior. The co-teachers determine whether the undesirable behavior that the student is manifesting (doesn't do homework, is late to class, has poor unit test grades) is academic or social. Then they discuss the student's weaknesses (low reading level, medication that inhibits sleep, poor memory) and the student's strengths (very social, likes sports and music, great listening skills). Focusing on the weaknesses allows the co-teachers to see how a disability may be contributing to the difficulty; focusing on the strengths gives the co-teachers an opportunity to use the abilities of the student to create an action plan. The co-teachers then decide on one or two actions that may change the student's behavior (individualize homework, implement a behavior chart with rewards, offer more review before unit tests). The actions are then monitored to determine if they are successful or need to be revised.

Professional development

Team building and co-teaching practices may not be a specialty of anyone at your school. And, sometimes it is easier for staff to accept the expertise of a person specializing in co-teaching. For any of those reasons, you may want to consider hiring a consultant to facilitate team building and co-teaching practices.

In practice. A consultant contracted to work during the summer with newly formed co-teaching pairs met with them for four half-days. The co-teaching pairs participated in a series of team-building exercises and were given prompts to discuss their general preferences regarding managing and teaching students. The pairs were also given vignettes that described issues that may arise in co-teaching situations and were asked to describe how they would resolve the problems.

Figure 3.2 | **Analyzing Academic and Behavioral Manifestations**

Student: Sara B.   **Co-teachers:** Ms. Lional & Mr. Laconti   **Class:** Global Studies   **Date:** 11/5

Step	Action	Analysis
1	**Identify Undesirable Academic or Behavioral Manifestations**	• Poor homework completion and submission
2	**Identify Underlying Student Weaknesses**	• Poor decoding skills • Poor writing skills • Sleep cycle affected by medication
3	**Identify Student Strengths**	• Very social • Good verbal communication skills • Loves music and sports
4	**Create an Action Plan**	• Review homework for discernable pattern related to homework completed versus not completed • Review homework assignments to ensure reading level is appropriate • Create homework assignments that allow Sara to answer orally when in class
5	**Evaluate**	• Homework assignments requiring long written responses were not complete • Homework assignments with short written responses were consistently handed in and satisfactorily completed
6	**Revise**	• Supply an organizer (e.g., Frames) to help scaffold longer written responses • Create guided essays for student to complete • Work on creating time for Sara to respond orally to homework

What qualities do co-teachers need to be successful?

Successful co-teachers have an unswerving commitment to have all students in the class learn and succeed, and they have an incredibly strong belief that teaching together is much more powerful than teaching alone. Having confidence in another person's content knowledge and learning strategies is essential to a successful partnership. Successful co-teachers also recognize the need to create opportunities for the atypical learner to access the curriculum in an inclusive setting. Co-teachers need to have flexibility, a strong work ethic, and the ability to share responsibilities with confidence.

After working with hundreds of co-teaching partnerships, we have discovered that there are no insurmountable problems if the co-teachers have mutual respect for each other's knowledge and a shared work ethic. Many co-teachers begin the year in a reluctant and skeptical manner, but they eventually realize that students need the support of two teachers because one great teacher just can't do the job in an inclusive classroom. Good communication is an essential co-teacher quality, and fostering a good foundation for that interpersonal communication may be started by discussing answers to these questions:

1. What is your best attribute as a person? A teacher?
2. What noise and activity level are you comfortable with in a class?
3. What are your usual homework and grading policies?
4. What time do you usually start and end the school day?
5. How do you like to communicate with parents?

Changing "you" questions to "we" questions will elevate the conversation from a "me versus you" level to a collaborative co-teaching level:

1. How will we plan lessons together?
2. How will we make sure that each of us is a responsible and respected teacher in the classroom?
3. How will we accommodate the diverse learning needs in the class?
4. How will we prioritize curriculum topics?
5. How will we go about thinking of the best ways to teach a topic?
6. What strategies will we use to increase student learning?
7. What are ways that we can assess the learning of our students?
8. How will we share the responsibilities such as grading and talking with parents?

9. How will we establish a class that respects individual differences?

10. How will we communicate and solve issues or conflicts that might arise as our year together progresses?

How do co-teachers know what to do?

Although at the forefront of research, universities are sometimes accused of lagging behind educational realities. This might just be the case when it comes to training preservice teachers in the complexities of co-teaching. McKenzie (2009) surveyed 53 undergraduate programs at institutions of higher learning in 25 states and found that while 95 percent of the colleges required a specific course in collaboration for special education majors, only 16 percent required a course for general education majors. Furthermore, there were few actual collaborative experiences provided between the general and special education majors. The result is that few beginning teachers, particularly general educators, receive training in co-teaching during their preservice work. More veteran teachers, both general and special educators, might have received even less information on co-teaching, having been educated in a preinclusion era.

When we asked teachers to rate the importance of training in co-teaching, most thought it was imperative to the success of the program and were often critical of administration for not providing training opportunities. Ironically, while wanting training in co-teaching, teachers who receive training often have difficulties applying suggestions to their classrooms. Professional development is fraught with difficulties. Single workshops on co-teaching, while popular, can be informative and perhaps even enlightening, but do they lead to improved and sustained practices in the classroom? Donhost and Hoover (2007) suggest professional development could improve teacher practices if elements of constructivism were employed. They recommend creating opportunities for teachers to acknowledge and reflect on their beliefs, biases, understandings, and misunderstandings, as well as providing environments for discovering and integrating new knowledge and learning. Single workshops make this process difficult, at best.

Coaching throughout the year by a consultant with expertise in co-teaching can be more beneficial than periodic workshops, but it can also be quite costly. Some coaching paradigms include initial workshops that focus on the components of co-teaching and monthly follow-up with the consultant. These monthly contacts may entail a visit to the co-taught classroom where the consultant observes students and co-teachers, and makes note of the lessons. The consultant and the co-teachers (and if possible the paraprofessionals involved) meet afterward, usually for 30 to 45 minutes, to discuss the lesson in terms of content, delivery, and student learning.

Periodic half-day workshops are also beneficial when used in conjunction with monthly consultations. The co-teaching pairs meet with the consultant to share experiences, learn from one another, and get introduced to more strategies. Likewise, since co-taught classes differ, visitations between co-teaching classrooms with time for discussions offer co-teachers the opportunity to see various models. We've found bringing co-teachers together leads to greater understanding of co-teaching, student needs, and curriculum components. In one such visit, 5th grade co-teachers observed a 4th grade co-taught math lesson. In the discussion that followed, the 4th grade co-teachers realized that they were expecting proficiency in areas beyond what the 5th grade teachers taught.

Professional development that involves workshops, classroom visits, debriefing, and co-teacher visits throughout the year furthers the collaboration process and gives ongoing support to the co-teachers. Districts that provide ongoing professional development send a strong message to co-teachers that there are high expectations and that the district is willing to support teachers' efforts toward excellence.

Given the financial obligations of ongoing professional development, it is important for administrators and supervisors to understand the complexities of co-teaching and assume supportive roles. Even when ongoing training is available, effective co-teaching ultimately rests on the professionalism of the co-teaching pair and a commitment to understand how students learn best.

As the expertise and knowledge of the co-teachers grow over time, how can they address changing expectations within their partnership?

Often overlooked is the progression of expertise of co-teachers. Co-teaching is so complex that it is quite unfair to expect expertise on curriculum, disabilities, and pedagogy right from the start. Gately and Gately (2001) developed a rating scale that segments the co-teaching relationship into three stages: beginning, compromising, and collaborating. These stages serve to highlight co-teaching as a dynamic and changing experience that requires both time and effort for a positive progression. The eight areas addressed allow co-teachers to differentiate between and focus on the complexities that form a relationship within specific areas including communication, curriculum knowledge, planning, presentation, classroom management, physical arrangements, and curriculum goals and modifications. There are two corresponding forms of the Co-Teaching Rating Scale, one for special educators and one for general educators. See Figure 3.3 and Figure 3.4 for the scales. While a score can be computed based on the responses, the survey is primarily used as a springboard for discussion and change. By sharing responses, the co-teachers can discuss agreements and disagreements across the areas and identify aspects that require attention.

―――――――●●―――――――

Case Study 5

How can we increase co-teachers' confidence in each other?

Mr. Salvatore, the general education co-teacher, did not volunteer for co-teaching. He is an accomplished science teacher, known for expertise and rapport with his students. Mr. Salvatore takes pride in his connections with students having the most difficulties learning. Although he thinks Ms. Mendoza, the special education co-teacher, is a nice person, he feels her presence does not add anything to the learning environment. Mr. Salvatore would rather go it alone and makes this very clear to Ms. Mendoza. Mr. Salvatore doesn't give Ms. Mendoza any chance to actively participate in the class and likes it when she sits in the back of the room and takes notes for students.

Statement of the problem

There is no parity of roles or responsibilities between the co-teaching partners. There is little understanding of the power that two teachers can offer in addressing the increasingly diverse and significant needs of students in an inclusive setting.

Problem genesis

The general education teacher is confident in his abilities and sees no reason to share the teaching.

Figure 3.3 | The Co-Teaching Rating Scale: Special Education Teacher Format

---

Respond to each question below by circling the number that best describes your viewpoint.

1: Rarely   2: Sometimes   3: Usually

1. I can easily read the nonverbal cues of my co-teaching partner.	1	2	3
2. I feel comfortable moving freely about the space in the co-taught classroom.	1	2	3
3. I understand the curriculum standards with respect to the content area in the co-taught classroom.	1	2	3
4. Both teachers in the co-taught classroom agree on the goals of the co-taught classroom.	1	2	3
5. Planning can be spontaneous, with changes occurring during the instructional lesson.	1	2	3
6. I often present lessons in the co-taught class.	1	2	3
7. Classroom rules and routines have been jointly developed.	1	2	3
8. Many measures are used for grading students.	1	2	3
9. Humor is often used in the classroom.	1	2	3
10. All materials are shared in the classroom.	1	2	3
11. I am familiar with the methods and materials with respect to this content area.	1	2	3
12. Modifications of goals for students with special needs are incorporated into this class.	1	2	3
13. Planning for classes is the shared responsibility of both teachers.	1	2	3
14. The "chalk" passes freely between the two teachers.	1	2	3
15. A variety of classroom management techniques is used to enhance learning of all students.	1	2	3
16. Test modifications are commonplace.	1	2	3
17. Communication is open and honest.	1	2	3
18. There is fluid positioning of teachers in the classroom.	1	2	3
19. I feel confident in my knowledge of the curriculum content.	1	2	3
20. Student-centered objectives are incorporated into the classroom curriculum.	1	2	3
21. Time is allotted (or found) for common planning.	1	2	3
22. Students accept both teachers as equal partners in the learning process.	1	2	3
23. Behavior management is the shared responsibility of both teachers.	1	2	3
24. Goals and objectives in the IEPs are considered as part of the grading for students with special needs.	1	2	3

Source: From Understanding coteaching components by S. E. Gately and F. J. Gately, Jr. *Teaching Exceptional Children 33*(4), p. 40–47. Copyright © 2001 by The Council for Exceptional Children. Reprinted with permission.

Figure 3.4 | The Co-Teaching Rating Scale: General Education Teacher Format

Respond to each question below by circling the number that best describes your viewpoint.

1: Rarely   2: Sometimes   3: Usually

1. I can easily read the nonverbal cues of my co-teaching partner.	1 2 3	
2. Both teachers feel comfortable moving freely about the space in the co-taught classroom.	1 2 3	
3. My co-teacher understands the curriculum standards with respect to the content area in the co-taught classroom.	1 2 3	
4. Both teachers in the co-taught classroom agree on the goals of the co-taught classroom.	1 2 3	
5. Planning can be spontaneous, with changes occurring during the instructional lesson.	1 2 3	
6. My co-teaching partner often presents lessons in the co-taught class.	1 2 3	
7. Classroom rules and routines have been jointly developed.	1 2 3	
8. Many measures are used for grading students.	1 2 3	
9. Humor is often used in the classroom.	1 2 3	
10. All materials are shared in the classroom.	1 2 3	
11. The special educator is familiar with the methods and materials with respect to this content area.	1 2 3	
12. Modifications of goals for students with special needs are incorporated into this class.	1 2 3	
13. Planning for classes is the shared responsibility of both teachers.	1 2 3	
14. The "chalk" passes freely between the two teachers.	1 2 3	
15. A variety of classroom management techniques is used to enhance learning of all students.	1 2 3	
16. Test modifications are commonplace.	1 2 3	
17. Communication is open and honest.	1 2 3	
18. There is fluid positioning of teachers in the classroom.	1 2 3	
19. I am confident of the special educator's knowledge of the curriculum content.	1 2 3	
20. Student-centered objectives are incorporated into the classroom curriculum.	1 2 3	
21. Time is allotted (or found) for common planning.	1 2 3	
22. Students accept both teachers as equal partners in the learning process.	1 2 3	
23. Behavior management is the shared responsibility of both teachers.	1 2 3	
24. Goals and objectives in the IEPs are considered as part of the grading for students with special needs.	1 2 3	

Source: From Understanding coteaching components by S. E. Gately and F. J. Gately, Jr. *Teaching Exceptional Children 33*(4), p. 40–47. Copyright © 2001 by The Council for Exceptional Children. Reprinted with permission.

How the problem is being denied or addressed

The general education teacher, through reputation and stature, is making it clear that the special education teacher is superfluous in this science classroom. The special education teacher, to avoid conflict, is taking a superficial role and relying on the general education teacher to meet the needs of the students. The special education teacher might have a tremendous amount to offer the students, but because she does not want to intrude, she is willing to let the general education teacher dominate.

Ways of promoting a positive outcome

• The special education teacher can begin to change the dynamics of this partnership by contributing behind the scenes. She can do error analyses of test responses and determine the types of errors students are making and share the results with the general education teacher. The special education teacher can also preview the curriculum and make up student-friendly review sheets and homework assignments. By taking these initiatives, it is likely that the general education teacher will see value in the special education teacher's input.

• By focusing on individual student needs and responses, the special education teacher can gradually shift the general education teacher's understanding about the importance of their partnership. The special education teacher can explain how learning differences affect students' classroom performances and how learning is enhanced by addressing the differences through different strategies and student groupings.

• The special education teacher should establish herself as a learning specialist and demonstrate that she has a firm grasp of the curriculum and may be able to change the general education teacher's attitude toward co-teaching.

• In some cases, the administration may need to take a more proactive approach by clearly emphasizing the importance of the partnership, causing parity to be achieved more quickly.

• The administration should emphasize that both teachers in an inclusive setting are responsible for ensuring that the needs of all students are being addressed by observing the class, meeting the co-teachers, and giving the co-teachers roles in the classroom.

Case Study 6

How can co-teachers get along?

Ms. Madaline and Mr. Jameson had a successful year co-teaching 7th grade language arts. They have confidence in each other's teaching abilities and knowledge of the subject. Observers could not tell which teacher was the special education teacher. Ms. Madaline and Mr. Jameson planned together, played various roles in each class, worked with students in groups, jointly created the exams, shared grading responsibilities, and contacted parents. Ms. Madaline and Mr. Jameson were considered the premier co-teaching pair, and other co-teachers came to observe how they worked in the class. After three years of co-teaching, Mr. Jameson went on a year-long child care leave. Ms. Landsing, a second-year English teacher who had also done some remedial English work with students, became Ms. Madaline's new co-teacher. Ms. Landsing was excited about her golden opportunity to work with Ms. Madaline in an inclusive setting. However, Ms. Madaline and Ms. Landsing never hit it off. According to Ms. Landsing, Ms. Madaline dictated how things needed to be done, constantly referring to how she and Mr. Jameson had done things. More often than not, Ms. Landsing left the class crying. Ms. Madaline felt superior to Ms. Landsing and couldn't understand her teaching methods. Ms. Landsing felt belittled and even a bit bullied by Ms. Madaline.

Statement of the problem

Although her initial experience with a co-teaching partner was positive, the special education teacher is having difficulty adjusting to a new co-teacher.

Problem genesis

Every co-teaching pair has a unique dynamic. There is no single right way to co-teach but difficulties arise when co-teachers don't discuss roles and responsibilities or establish a working relationship.

How the problem is being denied or addressed

The co-teachers seem to be on their own to solve this problem. Administrators aren't involved; despite the general education teacher's emotional responses, there seems to be little effort on either teacher's part to address the difficulties.

Ways of promoting a positive outcome

• Acknowledging that each teacher has unique strengths can go a long way to building a bridge between these teachers. Ms. Madaline, although missing Mr. Jameson, had a positive co-teaching experience, so we know that she can work well with another teacher in the room. Ms. Landsing's experiences, as both a language arts teacher and a remedial teacher, enable her to contribute greatly to the needs of the students.

• Identifying that there is a problem can be the beginning of a resolution. Neither co-teacher is happy with the situation, and they are having difficulties understanding the source of the problem and communicating in a positive way. They need to discuss the problem, including the reality that there is no single way to co-teach, and how two teachers go about it depends on their personalities, knowledge, and the dynamics of the particular class.

• Working independently, the co-teachers can rate the statements in Figures 3.3 and 3.4. Then they meet to share and discuss their answers. Conceivably, these co-teachers might find that they have more in common than they think and can work from a shared vision instead of differences and disappointments.

• The interactions between the co-teachers can become more positive if they begin to focus on the needs of their students. By looking at student needs and success, the teachers can work together for a common goal and redirect the attention from each other.

• The co-teachers can start to establish some routines in the classroom for which each is responsible. For instance, Ms. Madaline can continue to make up the tests (ideally, it would be done jointly), and Ms. Landsing can analyze the errors made by students who fail the quizzes and tests.

• Ms. Landsing must not depend on Ms. Madaline for all her knowledge of co-teaching. She must take more initiative and acquire some basic knowledge of co-teaching.

• While somewhat tricky to accomplish, some input from others could assist in this situation, and the co-teachers can benefit from involvement of a neutral other party. Although administrators can take on this role, the co-teachers might become defensive or hide the difficulties. Lead teachers or psychologists might be able to guide a change. Likewise, establishing professional learning communities with honest discussions can lead to open and positive talks on relationships.

• Leaving teachers to settle (or ignore) problems ultimately hurts the students. Either teacher could begin a conversation (or ask someone else to broach the subject) about how a poor co-teaching relationship can negatively affect students. With this sort of reminder, co-teachers may be more likely to address the source of the differences, settle them, or set them aside so that student growth and learning takes priority.

My co-teacher is the only person allowed to call me at 1:00 a.m. to discuss the next day's lesson!

—Middle school general education co-teacher

We are lucky that we are scheduled three periods each week to plan together.

—Elementary co-teachers

We knew in June that we would be co-teaching so we spent some of the summer co-planning and working out how we wanted the class to run. Come September, we really felt that we had things under control.

—Secondary school co-teachers

Unfortunately we do very little planning and my role in the co-taught class is minimal. I really feel like a teacher's assistant.

—Middle school special education co-teacher

Although we have some time during the day to plan together, we usually get more done on the phone. We both have a long commute, so every afternoon we talk on our cell phones about the day and what we want to do the next day. We even talk in the morning on our way in to school. We always go out for lunch and if you can believe it, we still like each other and get along great!

—Elementary school co-teachers

4

Planning Lessons

Mr. Tomas thinks about the year so far. It is the first year of co-teaching in 7th grade, and he is assigned to four teachers in four content areas. Six students classified as being in need of special education services are in his classes. Each day he sees these students in the content classes, meets with them for a support class, and preteaches and reviews the materials for each content class. That is the good part. The problem is the lack of planning time. Mr. Tomas and the four content teachers share a common preparatory period every day, but other issues consume that time. The guidance counselors often use that period to discuss students, and the team often makes parent calls or holds conferences. Keeping up with the four subjects without planning is nearly impossible for Mr. Tomas, and he imagines how much more effective he could be with proper co-planning with his team of teachers. As it is, he finds out what is going to happen each day when he enters each classroom. This can't be what co-teaching is supposed to be, Mr. Tomas thinks.

Ms. Longhorn meets Mr. Tomas by the doorway as students enter the room. She likes Mr. Tomas but doesn't see him as a responsible or active co-teacher. Ms.

Longhorn doesn't understand why she is responsible for planning each unit and each day's lessons, grading papers, and marking homework and tests. She even takes attendance. Ms. Longhorn thought that co-teaching this 7th grade class was going to be a partnership and is disappointed. During class Mr. Tomas walks around and assists students and occasionally interjects some thoughts. Ms. Longhorn feels, however, that Mr. Tomas could at least have the initiative to take attendance and take over some lessons.

Why do some say that without co-planning there is no co-teaching?

Although the relationship between co-teachers is thought of as foundational to the success or failure of a co-teaching partnership, only co-planning on a regular basis and in an insightful manner allows for the full, positive impact on student learning.

Obviously, we support co-planning and concede that an effective co-planning process requires a great deal of time, effort, and coordination. Complicating co-planning are situations in which the special education co-teacher is shared among multiple general education co-teachers, subject areas, and grade levels. It is not unusual (although not considered best practice) for a middle or high school special education teacher to be assigned to two English classes and two social studies classes, each co-taught with four different general education teachers. Many elementary special education co-teachers find their assignments split between two teachers and often grade levels. Special education teachers feel lucky if the classes are on the same grade level, or if their schedule remains the same for a few years so that they can better master the content. Understandably, effective co-planning in these situations is extremely difficult.

When co-teachers co-plan lessons, however, the integration of content and process (the what and the how of the lessons) become ingrained in the creative thinking of the co-teachers. They can incorporate essential elements of instructional and universal design (see Chapter 6) directly into the formation of the lessons so that the tasks and lessons are intentionally designed to teach the content to a diverse student population. Co-planning allows teachers to scrutinize the curriculum and make critical decisions about what needs to be covered, taught, and learned. They can incorporate big ideas throughout the curriculum and emphasize a depth of understanding.

Co-planning is difficult. Considering the logistical limitations that many co-teachers face, it is perhaps unrealistic to think that every lesson in every co-taught class will be co-planned. Streamlining the planning process and creating foundational routines that support intense instruction can help (see the next section on planning courses, units, and lessons).

Should both co-teachers be involved in the lesson planning, or does the general education teacher plan for the whole group and the special education teacher plan for the students with special needs?

Elemental to co-teaching is a partnership, and some co-teachers define this as sharing responsibilities. At times this translates into a division of labor and may result in assigning a group of students to one of the co-teaching partners. If this happens, the special education teacher is often responsible for the students with special needs, and the general education teacher is often devoted to the rest of the class. The assignment of teachers and groups could be for planning, teaching, or overseeing—or all three. This is a dangerous precedent, and the overuse of this quasi-alternative model of co-teaching and planning creates a virtual classroom within a classroom and may nurture stigmatization. In addition, nearly complete compartmentalization means that the students with special needs will not be exposed to the full curriculum, variations in experiences, or a broad range of thinking.

At other times, there are co-teachers who divide the curriculum. For instance, one co-teacher might plan for English and social studies, while the other plans for math and science. The division of labor may seem time-effective, yet the arrangement ignores both the shared decision making that consistently takes students' needs into consideration and the shared discourse that examines how and what is to be taught.

Unfortunately, many co-teachers fall into routines where the general education teacher is responsible for most elements including curriculum, pacing, lessons, test preparation, and grading. In these situations, the special education co-teacher's main contributions are to support students during the general education teacher's lessons. The one teach, one (minimally) support model of co-teaching dominates these lessons, and once again the power, efficiency, and effectiveness of co-teaching is severely diminished.

Co-teaching involves a commitment to co-planning, no matter how difficult, and preparing lessons together enables co-teachers to capitalize on each other's strengths, allows for intensive reflection on how to best meet the needs of the students, and creates co-teaching lessons that are extremely powerful.

When do co-teachers have time to plan?

The importance of planning time cannot be overstated, and to be effective co-teachers must schedule planning time during the school week. Administrators demonstrate that they value and support co-teaching by incorporating planning time into co-teachers' schedules, and they extend that support if they exchange duties (i.e., hall duty, lunch room duty) for common planning time. Co-teachers need at least two hours a week together to plan. Considering the complexity of planning in general and the components of co-planning, most co-teachers spend more than two hours a week planning, most often on their own time. Admittedly, most teachers plan well beyond the school day. But, if the administration does not acknowledge the necessity and demands inherent in co-planning, co-teachers may resent the extra efforts.

Even with scheduled planning time, co-teachers often find themselves planning before and after school, between lessons, over the phone, and by e-mail. Google Docs or Dropbox, which allow for multiple users to work on the same document, are great ways for co-teachers to work on lessons and assignments beyond the school day and building.

Although time together is important, even with expanded planning time (three times a week or daily), co-teachers may not use the time efficiently. Demands such as parent calls and meetings of the Committee on Special Education get in the way of co-planning. In addition, districts rarely offer an alternative (beyond the general lesson plan protocol) for co-teachers to use in planning for their unique student needs, content challenges, specific strategies, and co-teaching models. See page 61 for a description of a process that co-teachers can find useful in making decisions and communicating plans to supervisors.

Taking a slow and steady attitude about planning from the beginning allows co-teachers to cope with the demands of co-planning. Starting with thorough co-planning for a particular subject or unit and building up to multiple subjects or units is a realistic plan of action. As co-teachers spend multiple years together, the number of subjects and units co-planned together increase, so planning becomes less burdensome. In addition, concentrating on two co-teaching approaches in a marking period (for instance, parallel and station teaching) can benefit the teachers as they become familiar with the models and refinements to each.

How does understanding student needs affect planning for the class?

Special and general educators as co-teachers have a fundamental responsibility to students, and they should approach each lesson with this in mind. Simply asking how a particular student will go about attending to, completing, and learning the material starts the necessary reflective process. Co-teachers who use the Rating Scale for Teaching Materials and the Task and Lesson Rating Scale (see Chapter 6) are able to analyze materials and lessons with respect to individual student needs. The needs of the students are at the heart of the co-teaching program, and the scales will help co-teachers as they strive to understand the diversity of learners in their classrooms.

Is there a streamlined process to plan co-teaching lessons?

Co-teachers can use simple methods to monitor lessons, develop role awareness, and track student needs and progress. The Quick Co-Teaching Plan shown in Figure 4.1 delineates the demands of each day:

- Date
- Lesson's aim or essential question
- Sequence of student tasks (i.e., listen to lecture, answer questions orally, read, and write a response)
- Materials designed to meet student needs
- Adaptations and strategies to be used in delivering the lesson. Note that adaptations and strategies should be repetitive. For instance, once a particular reading strategy is introduced, modeled, and practiced (e.g., RAP; see Chapter 7) then it should be enlisted whenever students are reading.
- Selections of co-teaching models (one teach, one support; parallel; station, alternative; or teaming) for each task.

Figure 4.1 | The Quick Co-Teaching Plan

Date	Lesson's aim	Sequence of tasks	Materials	Adaptations and strategies	Co-teaching models	Student focus	Co-teacher reflection	Planning for future lessons
2/11	What contributed to the growth or decline of an early American colony?	Reading editorials comparing Jamestown and Plymouth	NY Times Editorial	RAP strategy for reading	Alternative	John (attention) Ramondo Juliet Stephanie (reading comprehension)	RAP strategy worked great. Continue to use when reading social studies material.	Make a word bank available for the categories in the adapted Venn diagram to elevate need for alternative model.
		Discussion			Parallel: Group 1 Jamestown; Group 2 Plymouth. Then Teaming			
		Written comparison of colonies	Adapted Venn	Adapted Venn diagram for comparison	Alternative	Stacy, Matt, Jack, Sonia (written expression and organization)	Students need more practice with adapted Venn	Use adapted Venn next week to compare colonial leaders
2/12								
2/13								
2/14								
2/15								

• Student focus. By preselecting a student for intense reflection each day, the co-teachers can focus on, talk about, and reflect on that student's needs.

• Co-teacher reflection. Did this lesson go well, or was it a bust? How could the lesson have been improved? Were other adaptations or strategies needed?

• Planning for future lessons. What needs to be done next?

What about a more detailed way to plan courses, units, and lessons?

The process of co-planning can be complex, yet it is essential for the incorporation of the elements required for successful instruction and learning. The first step is to have a co-teaching conversation that reveals the commonalities and differences between the co-teachers on their preferences regarding homework, discipline, and grading. Next, the general course elements that are covered throughout the year are outlined and discussed. A streamlined way to outline the year is to use the Co-Teaching Frame (Figure 4.2), a simple graphic with the course or unit in the center and the course units or lessons connecting to it along a time frame. Using the frame to guide the process gives co-teachers a simple structure for their conversations about planning for the year or unit.

The Co-Teaching Frame is a base for the general framework of the units, from which lessons are developed. As each unit approaches, the co-teachers delineate the unit into lesson topics or aims. The frame includes a time line and a brief explanation of co-teacher roles and responsibilities related to that lesson, for easy discussion and reference.

The layers of the Co-Teaching Pyramid in Figure 4.3 offer another approach that provides an illuminating guide for co-teachers as they co-plan. The pyramid incorporates the elements of student needs, effective instruction, co-teaching models, and lesson and material design described in this book. The pyramid has four basic layers or levels:

Layer 1, the base of the pyramid, is at the unit level. When beginning to plan a unit, the co-teachers think about the cognitive demands for students in the class. For instance, for an English unit focusing on reading and writing memoirs, the co-teachers discuss the literacy and skill demands of reading and understanding the memoirs assigned, and the skill prerequisites for writing a personal memoir.

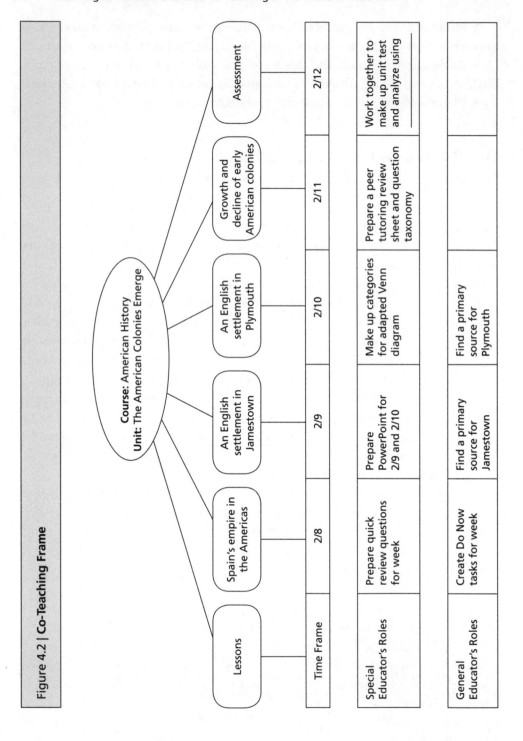

Figure 4.2 | Co-Teaching Frame

Course: American History
Unit: The American Colonies Emerge

Lessons	Spain's empire in the Americas	An English settlement in Jamestown	An English settlement in Plymouth	Growth and decline of early American colonies	Assessment
Time Frame	2/8	2/9	2/10	2/11	2/12
Special Educator's Roles	Prepare quick review questions for week	Prepare PowerPoint for 2/9 and 2/10	Make up categories for adapted Venn diagram	Prepare a peer tutoring review sheet and question taxonomy	Work together to make up unit test and analyze using _____
General Educator's Roles	Create Do Now tasks for week	Find a primary source for Jamestown	Find a primary source for Plymouth		

Layer 2 is at the lesson level. Look at the demands of the particular lesson, and ask what the challenges of the lesson are. Use the Rating Scale for Teaching Materials (Figure 6.5) and Task and Lesson Rating Scale (Figure 6.6) (pp. 104–105) to analyze the assignment and materials or to design materials that will be appropriate for the diverse needs of the specific students in your class. For the English unit on memoirs, the co-teachers discuss the reading difficulty of the preselected memoirs and decide if they will ask the whole class to read one memoir or offer a choice at different reading levels and appeal (e.g., sports, politics, or celebrities). When students are assigned to write a personal memoir, the co-teachers might do a task analysis of the assignment and structure the activity into scaffolded parts.

Layer 3 is at the instructional and strategy level. Co-teachers determine what essential element of instructional design is appropriate for the aim of the lesson based on the task demands analyzed in Layer 2, and which corresponding strategy or routine will be implemented (see Chapter 7). For instance, if the co-teachers decide to let students choose among memoirs, it is important that everyone understands the big ideas (essential components) of the memoir. Students use the Basic and Expanded Concept Formats (Chapter 7) to depict the schema of a memoir: title and author in the center circle with the four segments labeled (1) significant events in life, (2) challenges and accomplishments in life (3) how this person affects others and the world, and (4) how their chosen memoir addresses the essential element. Students then share their information on memoirs and compare and contrast the lives of the people they have studied.

Layer 4 helps co-teachers decide what most effective, efficient, and intensive co-teaching approach (see Chapter 2) to use so all students can access and learn the content. The co-teachers might use parallel teaching for comparing and contrasting the various memoirs. For example, one teacher would discuss the challenges that the personalities faced while the other would concentrate on the accomplishments.

In addition to using the frame and pyramid, some co-teachers find it helpful to plan backward by first creating quizzes and tests and then developing lessons. Backward planning helps teachers concentrate on the big ideas and essential questions of the unit and keeps the pacing of the class on target. Whether co-teachers develop the quizzes and tests before or after the lessons, exams that are user-friendly and have a balance of difficulty levels and depth will allow an assessment of students' actual acquisition of knowledge.

Figure 4.3 | Co-Teaching Planning Pyramid

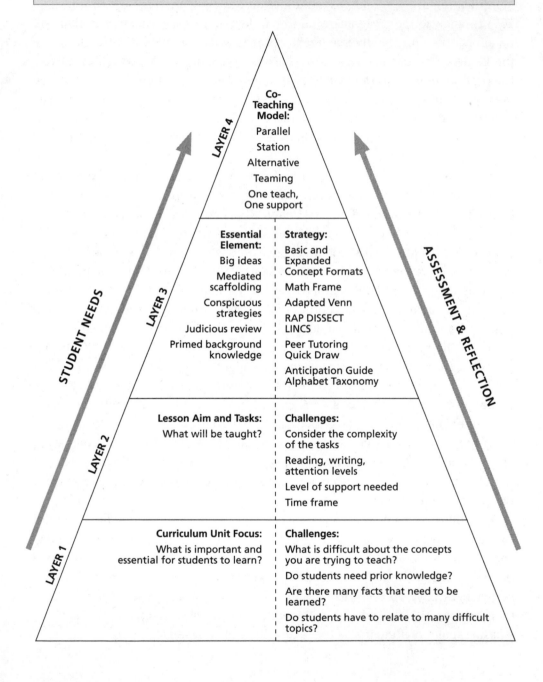

Special attention to homework assignments can also make a significant difference for students experiencing difficulties in the class. Co-teachers need to analyze the difficulty level (see Chapter 5 for information) and purpose of each homework assignment, and decide which homework assignments to differentiate so that students can work independently to reinforce important skills. Working backward to arrange the homework assignments so that they are review sheets for the quizzes and tests is a good strategy.

———————•●●————————

Case Study 7

How can we encourage co-teachers to plan together?

Mr. Matthews is a first-year middle school math teacher who is co-teaching with Ms. Susana, a veteran special education teacher. Ms. Susana has taught self-contained special education classes, was a resource room teacher, and was part of a co-teaching collaborative program in the middle school for three years. Mr. Matthews and Ms. Susana are part of a team made up of 7th grade content teachers (math, social studies, science, and English). Ms. Susana co-teaches two math classes each day with Mr. Matthews and two English classes with Ms. Robin.

Mr. Matthews is finding his first year of teaching a bit overwhelming. Although the district relieves co-teachers of one duty assignment (i.e., bus duty) so they can have a class period each day to plan, he finds that he needs time to think and plan alone. He hands Ms. Susana the plan and handouts each day, right before first period. Mr. Matthews's lesson plans are the same for the two inclusion classes and three solo-taught math classes. Ms. Susana is frustrated because she never knows what is going to be covered during the class, and she feels that the materials need to be designed to better meet the needs of some students.

Statement of the problem

The co-teachers do not plan together, and the needs of the students are not being met.

Problem genesis

The first-year general education teacher needs time to think and wants to plan lessons on his own.

How the problem is being denied or addressed

The co-teachers are at an impasse because the general education teacher insists on planning alone, and the special education teacher is hesitant to talk about the situation.

Ways of promoting a positive outcome

• The special education co-teacher may offer to design the Do-Nows or review sheets for the in-class assignment, relieving the general education co-teacher of some work and modeling how materials could better meet student needs.

• The special education teacher may insist on meeting at least once a week —if not to plan, then to discuss the performance and progress of students.

• Administration may require that lesson plans be submitted a week in advance.

• Administration may send the teachers to a professional development workshop on co-teaching that might spur a discussion between them related to their roles and planning.

• The special education teacher may introduce the Rating Scale for Teaching Materials and the Task and Lesson Rating Scale and discuss how the materials and lessons meet (or don't meet) the needs of the students.

• Impetus to change may come from the special education teacher or the administration, with an explanation that reinforces the fact that the behavior of one co-teacher cannot usurp the responsibilities of the other or the needs of the students.

———————————— ◄●► ————————————

Case Study 8

How can we support co-planning?

Ms. Hernadez, a general education 6th grade math teacher, is up for tenure this year. Teaching is a career change—she worked in the corporate world for 20 years. Ms. Hernadez is overwhelmed and anxious regarding her tenure and wants to be sure everything she is doing is absolutely perfect. She and Ms. Kim, a 10-year veteran special education resource room teacher, are co-teaching for the first time. Ms. Kim has never taught on the 6th grade level and is partnered with three other general education teachers for the other content areas (English, social studies, and science). Added to Ms. Kim's responsibilities is a district mandate to learn and use a new computer program for IEPs. These co-teachers use a one teach, one support model of co-teaching exclusively, and Ms. Hernadez does all the planning.

Statement of the problem

The co-teachers are not co-planning and consequently have diminished their effectiveness in the classroom.

Problem genesis

Both teachers are inexperienced at co-teaching, and the special education teacher has four subjects to learn while working with and accommodating four different general education teachers.

How the problem is being denied or addressed

Feeling overwhelmed and unsupported, the co-teachers seem happy to get through each class period.

Ways of promoting a positive outcome

• Administration can change the format for co-teaching from one special education teacher learning four subjects to two subjects (e.g., English and social studies, or math and science). Fewer subjects enable the special education teacher to become proficient in the subject matter and have more time to co-plan.

• One or both co-teachers or the administration can suggest that the co-teachers attend workshops or staff development on co-teaching with an emphasis on planning, or work with a consultant in a positive, nonthreatening manner.

• School administrators need to observe the co-taught class and give recommendations on using other models of co-teaching.

Pacing is a concern in co-teaching. I am really excited to co-teach next year, but I know my special ed partner wants students to know the material before moving on. I understand that but I really feel an obligation to the other students in the class to make sure that I cover the material.

—Elementary general education teacher

Planning with four general education teachers is really a problem. I know I could be so much more effective if we had one team of general education teachers in the 7th grade that had co-teaching inclusive classes, and if there were two special education teachers assigned to the team.

—Middle school special education teacher

Grading is a real problem. We don't want the parents to get the idea that their children are doing better than they really are in comparison with the rest of the class. But we also don't want to demoralize the students. Our report cards are based on a 4-point scale with 1 being deficient. At least 3 students with IEPs in our class are going to get all 1s on their report cards. It doesn't mean that they aren't making progress but their skills are still very deficient.

—Elementary co-teachers

5

Developing Curriculum and Assessment

Ms. Morgan gives the adapted unit test to three of the four students with IEPs in the co-taught social studies class. Although she and her co-teacher adapted materials to teach the curriculum throughout the unit by providing readings at a lower reading level and visually displaying the content with short video excerpts, these three students were still doing poorly on tests and quizzes. Ms. Morgan adapted the test by keeping one-quarter of the test identical to the original, but she highlighted and underlined important words and phrases. She changed another quarter of the original test by simplifying the questions, substituting easier words, giving three choices instead of the original four. Ms. Morgan then made up the remainder of the questions and focused on the basic facts and vocabulary.

Ms. Applegate walks around the room as the students in the co-taught social studies class take the unit test. One student in particular catches her attention. Patty has a significant learning disability with problems organizing both materials and her thoughts and often does not quite grasp the concepts being taught, but she is a hard worker, does her homework, studies, and occasionally even answers a question or two. Patty's IEP does not stipulate any testing accommodations, and she usually gets 70s on the regular exams. Ms. Applegate can't help but question the fairness of adapting tests. The students who get the adapted tests don't work nearly as hard as Patty and are getting higher grades. Ms. Applegate feels that the report card grades for the students given the adapted tests will now be inflated and not be a correct representation of their knowledge of the curriculum compared with the rest of the class. She also wonders if the adapted test adequately addresses the depth of the curriculum.

How do curriculum and standards affect co-taught classes?

Obviously, merely placing a student with special needs in an inclusive co-taught classroom does not guarantee successful learning. The general education curriculum encompasses goals, methods, materials, and assessment measures. The overlap among these components is enormous. It is difficult to separate curriculum, goals, instruction, strategies, and materials used to reach the objectives because all are intricately related—whether in the co-taught or general education classroom.

Basically, curriculum is what needs to be taught or covered in a particular grade or class during the academic year. Meeting curriculum demands from local, district, state, and national standards is particularly difficult in a co-taught inclusive class; decisions as to what to teach involve these directives and informed discussions between co-teachers. Some educators and parents worry that the curriculum in an inclusive setting will be simplified and that standards and expectations will be diminished. While watering down the curriculum to accommodate students with special needs is not advised, neither is covering a wide range of topics without tending to the quality and depth of knowledge and understanding. Ellis (1997) posits that as a result of teaching strategically and deeply, the curriculum actually is "watered-up."

Concentrating on essential elements

Teachers feel the pressure of ever-changing and increasing curriculum demands, and many try to simplify their work by using a textbook that subsequently becomes the curriculum. Using textbooks as curriculum creates dilemmas for a number of reasons.

Surprisingly, textbooks are generally written at a higher grade level than the grade level of students who use the text (Allington, 2002). So it's easy to understand that students who have reading and writing difficulties and are reading below grade level will be further disadvantaged when attempting assignments from a text that has content appropriate to their grade level but well beyond their reading comprehension. Going chapter by chapter and teaching all the information eventually becomes overwhelming to students in any class as the overarching concepts become lost and are replaced by a multitude of seemingly unrelated facts. When co-teachers customize the information, omit nonessentials, and concentrate on the big ideas and how these ideas fit into more complex schemas, more learning can take place. Understanding the basic elements of the curriculum and how they fit into an understandable framework enables students to relate the information in more critical ways.

Concentrating on the essential, as opposed to simplified, components can also give teachers more time to ensure that students fundamentally understand and learn the curriculum. We worked with 4th grade co-teachers who, only after communicating with the 5th grade co-teachers, realized that the math text included many more topics than were necessary. By eliminating the nonessential topics, these co-teachers were able to devote more time to the skills and knowledge essential to their students' progress. Allington (2002) studied the practices of effective special education teachers and found that rather than relying on a textbook, they used many levels of instructional resources, offered students choices, and provided individual instruction. Co-teachers certainly have the opportunity to use these practices, which offer optimal prospects for student learning, more often than solo teachers. When the co-teachers agree on what needs to be taught and to what degree, they then can devote attention to the *how* of student learning. If the curriculum is undefined, there is a tendency to cover too much while students actually learn too little.

Incorporating opportunities for intense instruction

Further complicating curriculum demands are district policies that insist on pacing schedules for reading, writing, math, and other core content subjects. All teachers, including co-teachers, are expected to keep up with specific time lines. Given the fact that many students with special needs require repeated instruction and many opportunities to reinforce skills learned, a set schedule presents a unique dilemma for co-teachers: stay on pace and have students move along without developed skills, or slow the pace and have students perform with strong skills. When co-teachers agree on the essential curriculum components, pacing schedules become less ominous.

The way to address curriculum time constraints is to incorporate many opportunities for intense instruction through co-teaching approaches such as parallel, station, and alternative teaching. While whole-group instruction gives the illusion of covering the material, by using other approaches, co-teachers can provide direct instruction and reinforcement and increase the opportunity for intensive learning. The smaller groupings also increase opportunities for student responses, allow for additional assessment, and increase student time on tasks. Although whole-group instruction appears to keep the students in step with the pacing schedule, it's just an illusion of coverage.

How do co-teachers address both the curriculum requirements of the class and the IEP goals of individual students?

Further complicating issues of curriculum is the necessity to address the goals set forth in each student's Individual Education Program (IEP). The IEP is the legal document that outlines the type and extent of services needed by a student with special needs, as well as a series of goals the district is obligated to address. Depending on the unique needs of the student, the goals can range from basic reading, writing, and math, to organization, attention, and self-monitoring goals, as well as required options for specific services such as occupational therapy or speech and language therapy. Typically there are many more goals than can reasonably be addressed; yet, if included in the IEP, there must be some attention to teaching and monitoring student progress on these goals. IEP teams, recognizing the "curriculum goals versus IEP goals" dilemma, are beginning to align the IEP goals more closely to the curriculum.

In the lower elementary grades

In the early primary grades (K–3), the curriculum is somewhat aligned with basic IEP goals. The early grades curriculum emphasizes the acquisition of reading, writing, and math skills. Making use of both heterogeneous and homogeneous groupings with parallel and station co-teaching approaches, students can receive focused instruction in these basic skills. Co-teachers may also elect to employ alternative groupings in which a small group of students can receive targeted instruction in reading, writing, or math.

A district's program model of co-teaching has specific ramifications. When the co-teaching program involves a special and a general education teacher together for the entire day, there are numerous occasions throughout the day to do short, concentrated minisessions to target specific skills. If, on the other hand, the co-teaching program consists of a special educator in the general education class for a specified period of time (e.g., half day or just a few hours), the co-teachers are seriously limited regarding intensive instruction with alternative groupings. If the special educator uses large portions of the time to remediate skills, the whole point of being in an integrated setting becomes questionable. Likewise, if time is not spent remediating basic skills, then students' specific goals as delineated by the IEP are not being met. Co-teachers also need to stay aware of the possibility of creating a class within a class by too frequently using alternative groupings and concentrating on specific skills with a particular grouping of students. The key is to make sure the groupings are flexible with easy movement between groups based on need. Alternating which teacher teaches the smaller group also contributes to the goals of an integrated setting.

In practice. A team of 3rd grade co-teachers successfully integrated intensive instruction and focused on IEP goals by creating intensive instruction during morning work time. Their instruction included four individual stations (journal writing, map work, silent reading, and computer reading games) and two teaching stations for guided reading and reading fundamentals. In the beginning of the school year, the co-teachers varied which group they worked with. As the year went on, and a small group of students continued to need fundamental reading, the special education teacher took over that group each day. She also had another group for guided reading. If the special educator had taken the most intensive reading group from the beginning of the school year, the group may have been stigmatized. With gradual changes to the groupings and the teachers, the groups functioned without any undue attention.

In the upper elementary grades

The discrepancy among students' skills becomes more apparent in the upper elementary grades, where curriculum in content areas such as science and social studies is expanded and the demands on student skills and knowledge increase. Adapting materials by adjusting reading levels or writing demands helps students acquire information. General reading, writing, and math skills are always part of the curriculum, so students with difficulties can still focus on and progress with the basics that are taught in the integrated setting. The question persists, though, as to how severe difficulties in reading, writing, and math are addressed in the co-taught upper elementary setting. In some models, co-teachers are expected to remediate skills within the general education class; in other models there is a period in the day where students with intense needs are taught in a separate setting by the special education co-teacher in order to focus on specific skills. Students also may experience pull-out sessions for reading, writing, or math instruction taught by other school personnel, such as a reading teacher.

Addressing the needs of students within the upper elementary co-taught class can be accomplished by using time and groupings creatively. A student with poor sight word skills might be taken aside by a teacher or paraprofessional for five minutes multiple times during the day to reinforce the sight words. Morning work can be adjusted and differentiated so that the focus is on reinforcing basic skills. During the upper primary grades, specialized software may be introduced to students to help them with word prediction, as well as text-to-speech and speech-to-text features to help them develop written expression skills.

In the higher grades

Addressing both curriculum and IEP goals is quite a challenge at any level, but it becomes increasingly difficult and problematic as content acquisition takes priority over remediation in the upper grades. As grade levels progress, the adaptations and modifications needed to give all students access to the curriculum also increase. Of course, reading, writing, math, and language skills are needed in all classes at all levels, and the best co-teaching pairs incorporate numerous strategies to help students increase their skills in these basic areas. Universities continue to help students develop learning strategies to increase reading recognition, reading comprehension, and written expression, as well as provide content enhancements that allow students, particularly older students, to learn content in more efficient and meaningful ways. Many programs at the secondary level include a segregated period in which there is opportunity for the special education teacher to preteach and review content and also work with students on specific IEP goals. It's been our experience that the curriculum of the integrated setting drives most of what is done in the support class, however, and IEP goals become less important than acquiring content knowledge.

What is the difference between adapting and modifying curriculum in a co-taught class?

Confusion among the definitions and use of accommodations, adaptations, and modifications is widespread. In fact, many times the terms are used interchangeably. But there are differences. Although *accommodations* may change the setting or method of presentation or response, they do not alter the curriculum or expectations. For instance, accommodations may include extending the time allowed for certain students to take tests. *Adaptations* are changes in materials that give a student access to information but do not substantially alter the curriculum or expectations, such as simplifying and enlarging the print or font size on a test. *Modifications* have the potential to alter the curriculum in minimal to substantial ways, including limiting the amount of information taught. Lee and colleagues (2006) add yet another category, *curriculum augmentation*, which includes devices (such as graphic organizers), and learning strategies, which, though not part of the standard curriculum, expand it.

The issues related to adapting and modifying curriculum present another important area for co-teachers to discuss, understand, and address. We have found it helpful to analyze how some co-teachers have addressed the issues of accommodations, adaptations, modifications, and augmentations. Implementation can be situational and wide open to interpretation. What is a modification in one instance might be an adaptation in another, and what one teacher thinks is an adaptation might be interpreted by another as a modification.

Adapted and modified: In a 9th grade global studies unit on world religions, co-teachers expected students to know the basic tenants of each religion, its origins, founders, and guiding books. In addition, they wanted students to understand the similarities and differences among the religions and how religions affect today's world. Two students in the class had significant difficulties in reading and written expression. The teachers adapted the curriculum by giving these two students reading materials on a lower reading level than the rest of the class. Expectations were not lowered, and the two students were required to know the basics of each religion, as well as being able to demonstrate the higher-order thinking and understanding expected of their peers. Both students had testing accommodations that allowed for someone else to read the test aloud and write their answers. Another student in this same class, with grade-level reading recognition skills, had significant cognitive disabilities and difficulties understanding complex concepts. The teachers adapted materials for this student and modified their expectations. While the rest of the students needed to know five religions, this student needed to learn only the basic facts of two of the major religions and how they were alike and different. The curriculum was both adapted and modified for this student.

Adapted: Co-teachers in a 4th grade math class presented a unit on charts and graphs that included pie charts, bar graphs, and line graphs. The students needed to be able to read each kind of graph, know when each is best used, and transfer data to the appropriate graph. The co-teachers supplemented the standard curriculum and expanded the unit to involve more complicated data and analysis. The co-teachers adapted the materials for students who had math difficulties by using data with low numbers and did not require all students to master the more difficult graphing. The co-teachers in this instance considered the adjustments to be adaptations and not modifications.

Adapted: The 8th grade English curriculum required students to write a five-paragraph persuasive essay. The students with written expression difficulties were allowed to use word processors as an accommodation. In addition, the co-teachers initially modified the curriculum by changing the requirements to a basic one paragraph essay. Their intentions, however, were to gradually build up students' skills to the required essay. Other co-teachers in the same school used a graphic organizer that scaffolded information for a five-paragraph essay. They required the students with written expression difficulties to fill in the organizer with short notations and then gradually built up to actual sentences and paragraphs. These teachers felt they were adapting, not modifying the curriculum.

As you can see, the practices of adapting, modifying, or augmenting the curriculum is subject to interpretation based on the reality that the terms can have multiple definitions, mean different things to various people, and are often used interchangeably. Valid but potentially different practices are exactly why co-teachers need to discuss and reflect on their practices regarding any adjustments to the curriculum and be vigilant in monitoring their own work. Appropriate differentiation between adaptations and modification takes on significance when it comes to grading.

What accommodations are used in the co-taught class to assist students in accessing the curriculum?

At the heart of accommodation is the intention to assess what students know. Accommodations are determined by the Committee for Special Education when developing the IEP. The accommodations are changes in the areas of setting, presentation, and response. Some of the most frequent accommodations extended to students who have difficulties processing and accessing knowledge, include lengthening time to take tests, reading tests aloud to students, providing a scribe, or administering the test in an alternate quiet setting. These accommodations do not alter the curriculum in any way and give students with disabilities the opportunity to display their knowledge.

What becomes somewhat tricky is that an accommodation in one instance might be considered an alteration to curriculum in another. For example, if the purpose of a particular math unit test is to determine a student's ability to understand and solve word problems and apply knowledge—and the student has significant reading and calculation difficulties—then reading the test to the student and allowing the use of a calculator are appropriate accommodations because the intent of the test is maintained. However, if the math test is designed to determine the student's proficiency and automaticity of math facts (such as times tables), then use of a calculator or extending the test-taking period are inappropriate accommodations. What are thought to be accommodations can, in certain circumstances, alter the intent of the assessment and become modifications. For example, if a test to assess reading comprehension is read to the student, the test then actually becomes a measure of listening comprehension, not reading comprehension.

At times, teachers, students, and administrators may feel that accommodations give students unfair advantage, which is the opposite intent of granting the use of accommodations to level the playing field. To confuse the issue of accommodations even more, allowable accommodations differ from state to state, some people have a general concern that accommodations are offered to students without sufficient documentation, and little research is available to verify the success of their use. Even so, misunderstandings can be avoided in the classroom if the co-teachers thoroughly understand which accommodations are appropriate for each particular assessment. Bowen and Rude (2006) offer important guidelines for appropriate accommodations that include those that are matched for both the teaching and assessment of curriculum, and that provide equal opportunities for learning and demonstrating knowledge. Accommodations fall into several categories:

Flexibility in scheduling and timing: Given to address slow processing or work rate, limited attention span or frustration levels, or limited physical stamina.

- Using extended time or changing how time is organized by giving breaks periodically or administering the test over multiple days, or
  - Altering when the test is given.

Flexibility in setting: Given to address limited attention or physical impairments.

- Offering preferential seating or separate location to administer a test individually or in small groups, or
- Providing adaptive equipment or furniture such as a study carrel or special acoustics to minimize extraneous noises or special lighting for students with visual impairments.

Change of method of presentation: Provided to address visual or perceptual difficulties, hearing impairments, processing difficulties, and severe reading difficulties.

- Revising test format (using Braille or large-print edition),
- Adding space between test items and/or increasing size of answer spaces or bubbles,
  - Reducing the number of test items per page,
  - Presenting multiple-choice items in vertical format, or
  - Presenting reading passages with one complete sentence per line.

Revised test directions: Provided to ensure that students understand the requirements of the tasks.

- Reading directions to students or writing in simplified language,
- Underlining or highlighting verbs in directions,
- Using cues such as arrows and stop signs on the answer form, or
- Providing additional examples.

Change in method of response through the use of aids or assistive technology devices: Provided to enable students to access information or to demonstrate knowledge by bypassing skill deficits while addressing physical disabilities, tracking difficulties, attention difficulties, and learning difficulties.

- Using an amanuensis (scribe) or a tape recorder to capture oral responses;
- Using computer or other technology assistance, such as iPads, iPods, Kindles, Nooks, talking word processors, or visual or auditory amplification devices; or
  - Supplying physical devices, such as masks or markers as placeholders.

Other accommodations: Provided to address attention difficulties, visual or motor difficulties, and memory difficulties.

- Focusing prompts to keep students on-task,
- Waiving spelling or punctuation requirements or allowing use of spell-check or grammar programs,
- Waiving paragraphing requirements, or
- Allowing use of calculators or arithmetic tables.

How are students with special needs evaluated and assessed in a co-taught learning environment?

One of the most controversial aspects of inclusive classrooms is grading. Understanding the curriculum and standards is of utmost importance. As student motivation is often directly tied to level of success, many co-teachers use accommodations, adaptations, and modifications that yield grades that might be inflated. On the other hand, a student's grades might be deflated if care is not taken to identify how knowledge is being assessed. Co-teachers must come to terms with how accurately the student's grade reflects actual knowledge and attainment of goals. So how do the co-teachers provide opportunities for success for students with significant academic difficulties while adhering to the pacing, content, and assessment demands of the general education curriculum? The answer is that it's not easy.

Keep in mind that grading is subjective. Districts rarely have a policy on how to grade student work, and teachers usually create their own algorithms of what constitutes a report card grade, using combinations of the following assessments with varying importance: homework, projects, quizzes, unit tests, progress, and effort. The relatively arbitrary computation of grades, and the varying difficulty levels of assignments on which grades are based, causes grading to be even more challenging for co-teachers and their students with special needs. In a 10th grade co-teaching English class, the general education teacher insisted on giving a 30-question quotation test for every novel read, a task that was nearly impossible for the students with special needs to study for and pass. Although this particular teacher never waived this demand (stating that she would not lower her standards), the question is whether this type of test addressed the standards and requirements of the curriculum.

Students who go into a co-taught class from a more restricted special education setting may be accustomed to earning high grades based on their performance on a modified curricula, individual progress, and effort. Their grades in an inclusive setting will be based on a comparative scale with typically achieving students and therefore might be well below previous report card ratings. Once again, keeping student motivation high through successful experiences, while giving grades that reflect learning in comparison to peers, presents a dilemma for many co-teachers.

A helpful way to prioritize content and assess students is based on the premise that "all students can learn… not all students should be expected to learn everything" (Schumm, Vaughn, & Leavell, 1994, p. 611). Consider that the curriculum is divided into three components: (1) what all students are expected to learn, (2) what most students will learn, and (3) what some students will learn. For example, when creating an assessment, ensure that 70 percent of the questions are able to be answered successfully by all students, 20 percent by most students, and 10 percent by some students. On a 20-question assessment, 14 questions should be answerable by all students, 4 by most students, and 2 by some students. See Figure 5.1 for a graphic representation.

(1) *All* students are expected to learn both the basics and higher-order thinking. For instance, in a social studies class, all students are expected to know the big ideas of exploration. The big ideas might include knowing the basic facts of which European countries explored the new world, the explorers associated with each country, and the reasons for the exploration. All students would also be expected to analyze the similarities and differences between the first colonies as well as understanding the effects of colonization on the new world. Using the Test Assessment Chart (Figure 5.1), co-teachers making up a 20-question test would create 12 questions addressing that content and levels of understanding. The questions would be formulated within a range of difficulty, from perhaps asking students to fill in answers from word bank choices (easier) to requiring students to analyze primary sources (more difficult). You can see on the Test Assessment Chart that co-teachers expected all students to successfully demonstrate their knowledge on questions 1 through 14, with questions 1 and 4

being relatively easy, questions 5 through 11 being moderate, and questions 12 through14 being the hardest.

(2) *Most* students would understand the effects of American colonization on Africa, with questions 15 through 18 (ranging in difficulty from easy to hard) addressing those concepts.

(3) *Some* students would investigate political and social underpinnings of each of the countries that were involved in exploration and colonization of the New World. Questions 19 and 20 address those concepts.

All students were exposed to the full range of information and higher-order thinking, but co-teachers ensured that all students mastered the most essential elements. The lines between the divisions of categories (all, most, and some) are dashed because there are no hard division lines; and individual students, depending on skill and interest, might learn different concepts from each section. The Test Assessment Chart is a simple way for co-teachers to formulate or evaluate their tests by prioritizing the curriculum and helps them to create balanced and fair tests.

Another way to use the Test Assessment Chart (Figure 5.1) is to map the difficulty of the questions after the fact. For instance, if 5th grade co-teachers were unhappy with student performance on a test, they could use the chart to consider the difficulty of the test questions. In such a scenario, analysis of the questions revealed 80 percent were considered hard and placed in the inner circle. The co-teachers also discovered that 50 percent of the test required a level of understanding beyond the 5th grade standards and therefore were placed in the *some* section of the Test Assessment Chart. The co-teachers realized that their test did not fairly assess student learning. They reformulated the test so that both the content and difficulty levels reflected their teaching and their expectations. After giving the revised test, the teachers discovered that their students did indeed know the material.

A framework specifically designed for using curriculum standards as a basis for grading students with special needs, Jung and Guskey's (2010) Model for Grading Exceptional Learners (see Figure 5.2) works perfectly when IEP goals are aligned with standards. A thorough knowledge of the curriculum and standards is required, and students are graded on the basis of product (i.e., exams, reports), process (i.e., effort, homework), and progress (i.e., individual growth). Jung and Guskey's five-step model provides a transparent action plan for grading students with special needs.

Figure 5.1 | **Test Assessment Chart**

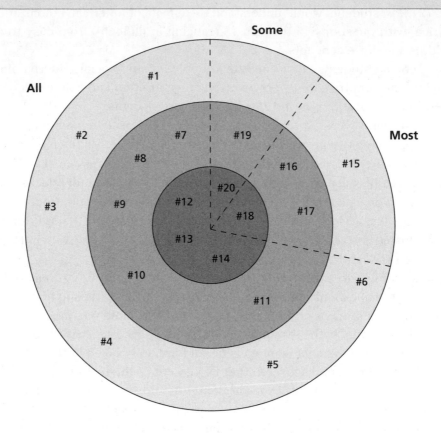

All students are expected to correctly answer questions at all three levels of questions.

The levels of questions   ☐ Easy   ▨ Moderate   ▨ Hard

All students are expected to correctly answer 70% of questions on the test (represented by questions 1–14)

Most students are expected to correctly answer an additional 20% of questions on the test (represented by questions 15–18)

Some students are expected to correctly answer an additional 10% of questions on the test (represented by questions 19–20)

Figure 5.2 | **Model for Grading Exceptional Learners**

Step 1: Ask whether the standard is an appropriate expectation without adaptations.

Step 2: If the standard is not appropriate, determine what type of adaptation the standard needs.

Step 3: If the standard needs modification, determine the appropriate standard.

Step 4: Base grades on the modified standard, not the grade-level standard.

Step 5: Communicate the meaning of the grade.

Source: Jung, L. A., & Guskey, T. R. (2010). Grading exceptional learners. *Educational Leadership, 67*(5), 31–35. © 2010 Lee Ann Jung and Thomas R. Guskey. Reprinted courtesy of Jung, L. A., and Guskey, T. R. All rights reserved.

Using this five-step process gives co-teachers an excellent guide to differentiate between adaptations and modifications and a means of communicating these decisions. Jung and Guskey also debunk certain long-held assumptions and myths regarding grading students with special needs, as noted in Figure 5.3.

How can co-teachers measure their success?

Research on the effectiveness of co-teaching in an inclusive classroom is difficult to synthesize. Students assigned to and served in co-taught classes often differ from district to district, and there is no apparent consensus as to what defines effectiveness. Does one judge success by student scores on high-stakes testing? Report card grades? Improvement in the areas being remediated? Individual achievement and growth or the achievement and growth of the group? Perhaps all components of success need to be considered. Two seminal articles (Murawski & Swanson, 2001; Scruggs, Mastropieri, & McDuffie, 2007) give meta-analyses of quantitative and qualitative research studies on co-teaching and conclude that more rigorous research on the effectiveness of co-teaching is necessary.

Clearly, research on the effectiveness of co-teaching is needed. We agree that consensus and informed parameters of exactly what to study would make researching the effectiveness of co-teaching more realistic. Ultimately, those involved in co-taught programs must evaluate the effectiveness in their individual settings based on the criterion that they determine to be important. When

---

Figure 5.3 | Myths About Grading Exceptional Learners

To ensure that the grades assigned to exceptional learners are both fair and accurate, we need to dispel these widespread myths:

Myth 1: Students with individualized education plans, students with 504 plans, and English language learners cannot legally receive a failing grade.

Fact: Any student, exceptional or otherwise, can legally fail a course. Legal provisions stipulate that individualized education plans (IEPs) must give students with disabilities the *opportunity* to receive passing grades and advance in grade level with their peers. If appropriate services and supports are in place and the appropriate level of work is assessed, then the same range of grades available to all students is applicable to exceptional learners.

Myth 2: Report cards cannot identify the student's status as an exceptional learner.

Fact: According to guidance recently provided by the U.S. Department of Education's Office of Civil Rights (2008), a student's IEP, 504, or ELL status can appear on report cards (which communicate information about a student's achievement to the student, parents, and teachers) but not on transcripts (which are shared with third parties—other schools, employers, and institutes of higher education) (Freedman, 2000). Even on report cards, however, schools must carefully review whether such information is necessary. There would be no need, for example, to remind the family of a student with multiple disabilities every nine weeks that their child qualifies for special education.

Myth 3: Transcripts cannot identify the curriculum as being modified.

Fact: This is perhaps the most common of all reporting myths. Under the Individuals with Disabilities Education Act (IDEA) of 1997 and 2004, Section 504 of the Rehabilitation Act of 1973, and the Americans with Disabilities Act of 1990, transcripts cannot identify students as qualifying for special services or *accommodations*— supports that provide access to the general curriculum but do not fundamentally alter the learning goal or grade-level standard. However, schools *can* legally note curriculum *modifications*—changes that fundamentally alter the learning goal or grade-level expectation (Freedman, 2000, 2005).

Myth 4: Higher grades equal higher self-esteem.

Fact: Probably the most dangerous myth is that students' self-esteem increases with higher grades. Most evidence, however, indicates that this is true only when grades accurately reflect students' achievement. When students receive inflated grades based on material that is not appropriate to their skill level, they actually lose motivation (Ring & Rietz, 2000).

Source: Jung, L. A., & Guskey , T. R. (2010). Grading exceptional learners. *Educational Leadership, 67*(5), 31–35. © 2010 Lee Ann Jung and Thomas R. Guskey. Reprinted courtesy of Jung, L. A. and Guskey, T. R. All rights reserved.

we ask co-teachers if they see growth in their students, they often look to report card grades and test and quiz scores to answer, which can give a distorted picture of student success. For instance, if the answer is that the student is passing or failing, we still don't know if his skills are actually improving or if the student knows the information. Students with special needs in co-taught classes often continue to have skill deficits when compared with typically achieving students. Judging to the norm might not recognize success when it is present.

The Co-Teaching Observation Guide (Chapter 8) asks co-teachers and supervisors to reflect on a series of questions to give evidence of student success. The following questions direct co-teachers to consider student participation and performance and to inspect the co-teaching methods that are used when teaching the curriculum.

- *Are struggling students answering and asking questions?* Co-teachers need to specifically plan for increased student participation to ensure active learning for all students by incorporating strategies that provide for judicious review (Chapter 7) such as quick drills, response cards, or simply thumbs up/thumbs down to increase participation.
- *Are students engaged in meaningful work throughout the period?* By careful planning and targeted teaching to student strengths and needs, co-teachers create meaningful tasks by incorporating models of co-teaching that provide for smaller groupings and adjustments of tasks based on student success or struggles.
- *How are teachers assessing the learning of each student?* Co-teachers can use exit questions (a question that students need to answer before leaving the class, usually related to an essential question of the lesson) for a quick and efficient way to access learning or can periodically use the one teach, one support approach or alternative model to specifically assess the levels of students' performance and understanding throughout the lesson.
- *What evidence is there that all students have been appropriately challenged?* Differentiating tasks demonstrates planning for the needs of all students in the class; incorporating Universal Design for Learning (see more in Chapter 6) elements with emphasis on engagement and choice encourages students to work at their appropriate level.

How can curriculum-based measurement help track the effectiveness of the co-taught classroom?

Consistent use of progress monitoring through curriculum-based measurement (CBM), when incorporated into the co-taught class, offers an efficient way to judge the effectiveness of co-teaching. CBM is a way to quickly and efficiently assess learning that is specific to a skill or curriculum. For instance, if a student's IEP goal is to increase reading fluency, the CBM would be a weekly or biweekly 1-minute test of reading where the number of words read correctly is assessed and charted. The difficulty level of reading passages used for the reading fluency CBM throughout the year is consistent so the growth in fluency could be ascertained.

Curriculum-based measurements are tests that are quick (usually 1–3 minutes), specific to a skill or curriculum, administered frequently (usually weekly or biweekly), and evaluated quickly with progress graphed. CBM can look cumbersome and complicated, but when streamlined to focus on specific skills, the process can be an integral part of the co-taught class and contributes greatly to knowledge of student growth (see Aldrich & Wright, 2001; Wright, n.d.).

Case Study 9

How can co-teachers determine the curriculum that is to be taught and assessed?

Ms. Tront, the general education teacher, and Mr. Lau, the special education teacher, are co-teaching a 5th grade social studies class unit on Egypt. Ms. Tront has visited Egypt several times, has tons of pictures, has read numerous books about Egypt, and knows the Egyptian section of the museum inside and out. As a result, this unit is one of the liveliest and most enriched units of the year, and the students gain a tremendous amount of knowledge. There are two quizzes and one unit test on Egypt, and the questions assess knowledge of the information presented. Although the students with special needs in the class enjoy the unit, they are doing poorly on both the quizzes and the unit test. Mr. Lau doesn't want to insult Ms. Tront, but she is expecting the students to know considerably more about Egypt than is required by the state or district.

Statement of the problem

Two problems need to be addressed in this scenario. The first is that the unit goes beyond the curriculum expectations. The second is that the special education co-teacher doesn't know how to talk with the general education teacher about the content expectations.

Problem genesis

Too much of a good thing can cause problems. Although Ms. Tront's knowledge and enthusiasm about Egypt make the lessons exciting, the problem lies in expecting and assessing students on the expanded and enriched curriculum.

How the problem is being denied or addressed

The problems are not being addressed, and students are being assessed unfairly because the extended curriculum isn't required of other students—and these students are receiving grades based on material that didn't have to be learned. Although the co-teachers have a positive relationship, this is a sensitive issue, and Mr. Lau is reluctant to approach Ms. Tront.

Ways of promoting a positive outcome

• Mr. Lau can talk to Ms. Tront, expressing both his enthusiasm for the unit and praise for her expertise while voicing his concerns regarding the assessments.

• Mr. Lau can start the conversation by looking over the students' responses and analyzing the errors. Using the Test Assessment Chart in Figure 5.1, the co-teachers can decide what material is essential for all students to know, for most, and for some. They can then assess the questions and see that the assessments went beyond the scope of the curriculum.

• Mr. Lau could get copies of the other 5th grade assessments on the Egypt unit and compare the expectations of the varying tests with Ms. Tront.

————————•●•————————

Case Study 10

How can we cover curriculum and ensure students are learning the material?

Ms. Ralp and Mr. O'Hare are co-teaching the first year of a two-year global studies course. The curriculum is demanding and fast-paced, and the co-teachers must ensure that they cover the material because the students will be taking a state exam at the end of the second year. They primarily use the one teach, one support model of co-teaching because they want all the students to get the same information, and they feel that lectures are the most efficient way of disseminating information. Unfortunately, many students, particularly those with special needs, are having difficulty understanding and remembering all the information.

Statement of the problem

Students are having difficulty learning the content taught.

Problem genesis

Emphasis on the curriculum can lead to inefficient and ineffective teaching. The content and pacing of the curriculum are creating a "cover it" rather than "learn it" environment in this co-teaching course.

How the problem is being denied or addressed

The co-teachers realize that they are moving much too fast for some students to learn, but they don't want to keep the other students from being exposed to the entire curriculum.

Ways of promoting a positive outcome

• The co-teachers need to take a thorough look at the curriculum and decide on the overarching big ideas and the most effective ways to teach them.

• The curriculum will be more manageable if the co-teachers determine what information needs to be understood by all, most, and some students.

• Looking at quiz and unit test items and determining what students know— and what is misunderstood—will allow the co-teachers to efficiently reteach material.

• Ms. Ralp and Mr. O'Hare should consider using other co-teaching approaches. They may find that teaching to smaller groups through parallel and station teaching will enable them to better teach the material.

I use a lot of the materials that my co-teacher designs for the inclusion class with my other classes. I'm learning to think a bit differently when I plan a task. I think about the students and how hard it might be for some of them. I'm using fewer published materials and designing my own.

—*High school general education co-teacher*

We break into stations or parallel groups almost every day. By placing students' names on charts hung around the room, even using different groupings, our students move to the correct area in a few seconds. It's an easy and quick transition.

—*Elementary school co-teachers*

My co-teacher really wants to teach the class on her own, although I'm certified in special education and science. I decided to start making up review materials and Do Nows. Bit by bit, my co-teacher is using the materials. I think she sees how hard I am working and how much I want to be an integral part of the team.

—*Middle school special education co-teacher*

I never realized that the way I constructed an exam would affect a student's grade. My co-teacher taught me how to format a user-friendly exam.

—*High school general education co-teacher*

6

Combining Instructional Elements, Materials, and Environment

Mr. Boez and Ms. Grant discuss the upcoming science project. They remember being disappointed by the projects their students submitted last year. This year, their second year co-teaching, they are determined to do things differently. Last year some students had a difficult time even coming up with an experiment, others attempted to do projects that were just too difficult, and the rest had difficulty allocating sufficient time for the experiment. Ms. Grant and Mr. Boez decide to keep students on track by scaffolding the project with interim deadlines for components of the project. In addition, they set a schedule for weekly in-class conferences with each student and added options for how students could present their projects. They realize that there is great diversity within the class in both ability and talent and want to give their students an opportunity to shine. Mr. Boez and Ms. Grant are confident that the quality of work will be high this year.

Sam, a student with learning disabilities, looks at the assignment sheet describing the science project. Last year he had to do an experiment using the scientific method, showing the steps and results on a display board. He remembered waiting until the last minute to do the project and realizing all too late that the experiment couldn't be rushed. Although he worked on it for the entire weekend before it was due, he never handed any of it in and got a zero on the project. That grade affected his final grade, and he almost failed for the year. Sam is determined to do better this year but doesn't quite know how. As he looks at the assignment, he notices something different. Included with the directions is a calendar with highlighted dates, indicating when different parts of the project are due. In addition, each week he has an in-class conference with one of his co-teachers to discuss how the project is going, as well as a few choices as to how he can present his results—a PowerPoint presentation, a video, or a traditional presentation board. Sam thinks that maybe he has a chance this year to do a good job.

What student needs must co-teachers address when teaching and designing materials?

The range of disabilities in a co-taught class can be daunting to understand and address, and co-teachers can gain an initial understanding of their students' special needs by accessing the information contained in the Individual Education Program (IEP). The IEP delineates the student's classification and its supporting evidence, outlines the necessary accommodations, and specifies annual goals that need to be addressed. The IEP is a written statement that is created collaboratively by the members of the Committee for Special Education (CSE), which includes the child's parents; a general education teacher; a special education teacher; a school representative; other experts, if necessary; and the child, if appropriate. At the beginning of the year, co-teachers read and discuss a student's IEP, but details of this information are often forgotten as the year progresses. Using a graphic organizer, such as the IEP Express shown in Figure 6.1, allows co-teachers to quickly reference a student's strengths, needs, IEP goals, modifications, and accommodations, as they work to reflect on and address the particular needs and goals of each student. If co-teachers fill out the information on large index cards and attach them to a file folder, the cards will work as a flip chart to keep the individual learning needs of students in focus throughout the year. The back of the card can be used for annotations and to monitor student progress. Some co-teachers make a card for each student in the class and substitute the different categories, such as Interests for Accommodations and Goals for IEP Goals.

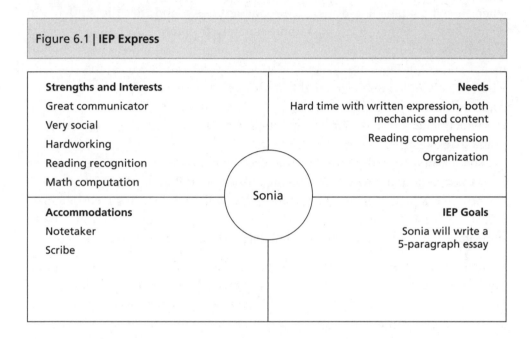

Figure 6.1 | IEP Express

Strengths and Interests	Needs
Great communicator	Hard time with written expression, both mechanics and content
Very social	Reading comprehension
Hardworking	Organization
Reading recognition	
Math computation	

Sonia

Accommodations	IEP Goals
Notetaker	Sonia will write a 5-paragraph essay
Scribe	

Which students with special needs are best served in a co-taught class?

Inspections of IEPs of students enrolled in co-taught classes reveal that there is no single profile for a student with special needs in a co-taught class. Participants in the CSE must decide and agree that the co-taught setting will meet the needs of the student and discount alternative placements such as

- a general education setting without support,
- a general education setting with resource room support,
- a general education setting with direct or indirect consultant services, and
- a self-contained or significantly separate placement.

The co-taught setting is considered an intense instructional placement within the most typical environment. In general, students who are classified and attend co-taught classes have more severe impairments than students enrolled in resource rooms or consultant services. A study that compared students who were classified in co-taught secondary settings with students who were classified in self-contained and resource room settings found that the students in co-taught classes had IQ scores approximately 9 points lower than students in resource rooms (Wilson et al., 2011). Although having more severe impairments and requiring more accommodations and related services, the students who were classified in the co-taught classes performed as well as their resource room counterparts on report card grades. These findings give some support to the effectiveness of co-teaching, although we acknowledge the subjectivity of grading and testing.

The learning and behavioral characteristics of students in co-taught classes are both many and varied. The manifestations of different classifications frequently overlap, so it is less important to know if a student has a certain classification (such as a learning disability or a behavioral disability) and more important to know what particular difficulties the student is experiencing.

• Students with reading needs may have difficulties recognizing or deciphering words (decoding), reading at a fluid and efficient pace (fluency), and understanding what is read on factual to interpretive levels (encoding).

• Students with language needs may experience difficulties listening to and retaining information (receptive language), interpreting and making sense of what is said (linguistic processing), and orally expressing thoughts through speaking (expressive language).

• Students with writing needs may have difficulties with the mechanics of writing (handwriting, grammar, spelling, punctuation) and the writing process (organized expression of thoughts through writing).

• Students with math needs may have difficulties remembering number facts and logarithms, and deciphering and completing application problems.

• Students with difficulties in learning efficiency may have difficulties originating or using learning strategies, keeping up with the pace of instruction, and transitioning between activities (flexibility).

• Students with attention issues may have difficulty focusing and sustaining concentration on tasks.

• Students with difficulties related to memory may not be able to retain information for a sufficient amount of time to process information (short-term memory), or store and retrieve information over time (long-term memory).

- Students with organizational difficulties may have a hard time keeping track of materials, schedules, and work, as well as organizing their thoughts for writing and conversing.
- Students with perceptual difficulties may misread or inefficiently process visual and auditory information.
- Students with metacognition difficulties may be inefficient at monitoring their learning, finding errors in their work, or reflecting on thinking.
- Students with difficulties making connections may have trouble relating what is known (background knowledge) to what is unknown (as they work to acquire new knowledge).
- Students with emotional or behavioral issues may have difficulties sustaining appropriate attention levels or following routines and rules.
- Students with social cognition difficulties may have trouble picking up nonverbal clues from others and situations around them.

What elements of effective instructional design are essential to support students with special needs in co-taught settings?

We've known for many years that the elements of good, effective teaching also work well for students with special needs. Ellis and Worthington (1994) summarize the research in 10 basic principles. In Figure 6.2 we synthesize their research and highlight the key concepts for students with special needs in co-teaching settings. Co-teachers who understand the rationale for effective instructional design are better able to translate the principles into practices that work for students with special needs.

Researchers at the University of Oregon provide guidance as to the essential elements of instructional design that specifically address the learning needs of struggling learners (Simmons & Kame'enui, 1996). These six elements fit well with the effective instructional design principles and provide a sound framework for co-teachers as they create an environment in which all students learn.

Big ideas address the needs of students to understand the overarching ideas and the specifics within topics. Many students have difficulty deciphering the main idea from the details and give all information equal importance. Instruction that highlights big ideas and shows how details and examples fit into the overarching theme provides many students with special needs a framework for

Figure 6.2 | Elements of Effective Teaching

Effective Teaching Principles*	Key Concept	Why Is This Important for Students with Special Needs?
Principle 1: Students learn more when they are engaged actively during an instructional task. (p. 15)	Students need to be active and engaged.	Many students with special needs are passive learners, and learning is inefficient and often incomplete. Therefore, their learning has many gaps in knowledge and misinterpretations of content.
Principle 2: High and moderate success rates are correlated positively with student learning outcomes, and low success rates are correlated negatively with student learning outcomes. (p. 17)	Students need to be successful.	Students with special needs in inclusive classes are expected to keep up with typically achieving students. When learning is taught and assessed in steps, students can be successful in increments and encouraged to persevere.
Principle 3: Increased opportunity to learn content is correlated positively with increased student achievement. Therefore, the more content covered, the greater the potential for student learning. (p. 22)	Students need to be exposed to content and have sufficient time to learn.	Historically, students in segregated special education settings were exposed to a limited amount of content. Students in inclusive classes now have the opportunity to be exposed to content that is greater in scope and substance.
Principle 4: Students achieve more in classes in which they spend much of their time being directly taught or supervised by their teacher. (p. 27)	Students need to be taught content directly.	Although a constructivist approach to learning provides a rich and varied experience for most students, many students with special needs have difficulty discovering relationships and generalizing concepts, and require information to be taught directly.
Principle 5: Students can become independent, self-regulated learners through instruction that is deliberately and carefully scaffolded. (p. 30)	Students need scaffolded instruction that leads to independence.	Many students with special learning needs require information to be sequenced and scaffolded, to give them better access to the concepts being taught.

Figure 6.2 | **Elements of Effective Teaching—(*continued*)**

Effective Teaching Principles	Key Concept	Why Is This Important for Students with Special Needs?
Principle 6: The critical forms of knowledge associated with strategic learning are (a) declarative knowledge, (b) procedural knowledge, and (c) conditional knowledge. Each of these must be addressed if students are to become independent, self-regulated learners. (p. 36)	Students need to learn how to systematically and efficiently acquire, demonstrate, and monitor knowledge.	Many students with special learning needs continue to use ineffective learning strategies.
Principle 7: Learning is increased when teaching is presented in a manner that assists students in organizing, storing, and retrieving knowledge. (p. 38)	Students need organized materials that assist memory.	Many students with special learning needs can use strategies for efficient learning but cannot initiate use of the strategies.
Principle 8: Students can become more independent, self-regulated learners through strategic instruction. (p. 59)	Students need strategic instruction.	Scaffolded and precise teaching enables students with learning needs to acquire and understand material.
Principle 9: Students can become independent, self-regulated learners through instruction that is explicit. (p. 68)	Students need explicit instruction.	Although many students with learning needs cannot initiate use of their own effective learning strategies, they can learn and use explicitly taught content.
Principle 10: By teaching sameness both within and across subjects, teachers promote the ability of students to access potentially relevant knowledge in novel problem-solving situations. (p. 72)	Students need to generalize knowledge to new situations.	Many students with special learning needs have difficulty accessing their knowledge and generalizing what they know to new situations.

*The Effective Teaching Principles (column 1) are adapted from Ellis and Worthington (1994).

understanding, remembering, and applying knowledge. Focusing on big ideas also assists co-teachers in planning and understanding content. By identifying and focusing on the comprehension of the big ideas and essential elements of the curriculum, the co-teachers enhance communication, understanding, and instruction.

Primed background knowledge requires co-teachers to connect what is being learned to students' experiences or former learning and accentuates the need to teach or prime the foundations for understanding the curriculum. Co-teachers who focus on the need to prime or teach information so that the students can make connections to the current content ensure that students are ready to learn the new material.

Conspicuous strategies consider the learning efficiency of students. Many students with learning difficulties have a tough time initiating effective and efficient strategies for learning but, if overtly taught, can successfully manage the strategies. Co-teachers can enhance successful learning by explicitly explaining the strategy and teaching it in stages as they model it, move students to independent practice, and finally help students generalize the use of the strategy.

Mediated scaffolding addresses the need of some students with learning difficulties to be guided to higher levels of thinking and understanding. A properly scaffolded lesson enables students to demonstrate cognitive strengths. Co-teachers include scaffolding in their lesson structures and frameworks to assist students in the acquisition and synthesis of curriculum, as well as to gradually support independent learning.

Judicious review acknowledges the memory deficits of many students with learning difficulties. Instead of bemoaning the fact that students don't remember or spend enough time studying, co-teachers incorporate memory strategies and repetition as integral parts of instruction.

Strategic integration puts all of the elements together into cohesive routines used across topics and disciplines.

How can Universal Design for Learning be used in a co-taught class?

Universal Design for Learning (UDL) provides a wonderful framework for instruction and material designs. UDL has its roots in an architectural movement to create environments accessible to all people from the inception of design. Rather than retrofitting buildings to provide accessibility, for example, universal designers incorporate accessible features from the onset. UDL extends the principles to the educational setting. Three fundamental principles guide UDL:

1. Provide multiple means of representation,
2. Provide multiple means of expression, and
3. Provide multiple means of engagement. (Center for Applied Science Technology [CAST], 2008)

Following UDL precepts in an inclusive classroom provides all students with multiple ways to access information, demonstrate knowledge, and become independent thinkers. UDL takes away the deficit disability model and adopts a diversity model that acknowledges the wide range of abilities, aptitudes, styles, and needs of all learners—a goal of co-teaching. The components for effective instruction for students with and without special needs run throughout the guidelines and are readily apparent in the Universal Design for Learning Guidelines shown in Figure 6.3. Choice is also an integral part of UDL, as is evident in Figure 6.4, an outline provided for creating your own UDL lesson plans.

How do co-teachers design materials that address student needs in co-taught settings?

UDL guidelines notwithstanding, co-teachers must thoroughly understand each child's strengths and weaknesses to appropriately design materials for an inclusive class. The more independent the task, the more likely it will need adaptation. For example, if some students have difficulties with reading recognition skills and the co-teachers opt to teach in stations, one co-teacher may read the text to a small group. Likewise, co-teachers might decide to pair stronger readers with the less proficient readers in an independent station. However, if the station task is to be done independently by each student, the co-teachers would need to adapt or design different materials. For instance, if the students who have significant difficulties with reading recognition skills are expected to read independently, they may be given materials that cover the same content as others but at a lower reading level or use text-to-speech software programs that will read the material to them.

One way of critically assessing materials to decide if adaptations are needed is the Rating Scale for Teaching Materials (Figure 6.5). Oftentimes, published materials overlook the intrinsic demands of the task. By using this rating scale,

Figure 6.3 | Universal Design for Learning Guidelines

Provide multiple means of representation	Provide multiple means of action and expression	Provide multiple means of engagement
1. Provide options for perception • Options that customize the display of information • Options that provide alternatives for auditory information • Options that provide alternatives for visual information	**4. Provide options for physical action** • Options in the mode of physical response • Options in the means of navigation • Options for accessing tools and assistive technologies	**7. Provide options for recruiting interest** • Options that increase individual choice and autonomy • Options that enhance relevance, value, and authenticity • Options that reduce threats and distractions
2. Provide options for language and symbols • Options that define vocabulary and symbols • Options that clarify syntax and structure • Options for decoding text or mathematical notation • Options that promote cross-linguistic understanding • Options that illustrate key concepts non-linguistically	**5. Provide options for expressive skills and fluency** • Options in the media for communication • Options in the tools for composition and problem solving • Options in the scaffolds for practice and performance	**8. Provide options for sustaining effort and persistence** • Options that heighten salience of goals and objectives • Options that vary levels of challenge and support • Options that foster collaboration and communication • Options that increase mastery-oriented feedback
3. Provide options for comprehension • Options that provide or activate background knowledge • Options that highlight critical features, big ideas, and relationships • Options that guide information processing • Options that support memory and transfer	**6. Provide options for executive functions** • Options that guide effective goal-setting • Options that support planning and strategy development • Options that facilitate managing information and resources • Options that enhance capacity for monitoring progress	**9. Provide options for self-regulation** • Options that guide personal goal-setting and expectations • Options that scaffold coping skills and strategies • Options that develop self-assessment and reflection

Source: CAST. (2008). *Universal Design for Learning guidelines version 1.0.* Wakefield, MA: Author.

Figure 6.4 | Universal Design for Learning Lesson Planner

Teacher(s): _____

Date: _____   **Subject:** _____

Standard/Benchmark/Indicator: Are you aligning your lesson with district or state standards? (Refer to applicable standards and performance indicators and list or distill here.)

Behavioral Objective: Student will...

Materials Needed: *(list items needed for the lesson)*

Multiple Means of Representation: How are you going to present your content so that it meets the needs of all students? Is the information represented in different ways? For example, you may use guided notes and graphic organizers in addition to a lecture format or use several books that represent different reading levels.

Multiple Means of Engagement: How are you going to provide multiple pathways for students to learn the material presented? Practice, or active mental or physical engagement, is required by students to make real learning happen. For example, some students may benefit from small-group learning opportunities, other students may require focused practice with precise feedback, and still others may benefit from working independently.

Multiple Means of Expression: How will students demonstrate what they have learned? Again, offering or creating many pathways to demonstration of mastery is key. Traditional tests, tiered assignments, and oral exams are some options. Also, multiple means of expression may be demonstrated by students building models, making videos, and creating portfolios.

Procedures: (What the teacher and students are expected to do in sequential order):

1. Activating Prior Knowledge: How are you going to motivate your students? Assess or review prior knowledge? Introduce the topic? Organize the lesson for students?

2. Teacher Modeling: Teacher demonstration of the strategy to be learned.

3. Guided Practice: Planned practice of the strategy under the watchful eye of the teacher.

4. Independent Practice: Planned options for students to demonstrate their ability to meet the behavioral objective.

Assessment: How you will assess students' products or "expressions." How will you know that the student understands the concept, got the idea, and can make applications to the process?

Source: © 2010 E. Blue, Hofstra University. Adapted with permission.

co-teachers analyze the material from the vantage point of generic characteristics such as reading level and interest level and customize the activity appropriately.

A more intensive way of looking at materials and lessons is through the eyes of students with specific difficulties. The Task and Lesson Rating Scale in Figure 6.6 is designed to help co-teachers focus on the difficulty of the task or lesson for students with particular academic difficulties and decide how to adapt the material or the mode of presentation. To personalize the scale and focus on specific students in the class, the co-teachers could insert the student's name in place of the generic *student* in the table.

Figure 6.5 | Rating Scale for Teaching Materials

Directions: Analyze the difficulty of the task or material for a student who is typically achieving. A 3 represents an appropriate level for the grade. If your task rates very high or very low, you may need to restructure it. Consider the following aspects of the task:

Aspect	Low end	Scale	High end
User-friendly. Is the format of this material designed to be accessible?	Simple	1 2 3 4 5	Complex
Reading level. Is the reading level of this material appropriate for the grade level?	Easy	1 2 3 4 5	Hard
Writing level. Are the writing demands appropriate for the grade level?	Easy	1 2 3 4 5	Hard
Attention. What level of sustained attention is needed for this task or material?	Low	1 2 3 4 5	High
Independence. What level of independence is needed for this task or material?	Low	1 2 3 4 5	High
Interest. How interesting is the task or material?	Low	1 2 3 4 5	High
Knowledge level. What amount of prior or newly acquired knowledge is needed for this task or material?	Little	1 2 3 4 5	A lot
Cognitive level. What level of thinking is required for this task or material?	Low	1 2 3 4 5	High
Importance. How important is this activity to the overall curriculum?	Low	1 2 3 4 5	High
Time. How much time is needed to complete this task? (Minutes)	Little	10 20 30 40 >50	A lot

Figure 6.6 | Task and Lesson Rating Scale

Consider and rate the level of difficulty of the task or the lesson for students with the following characteristics. Discuss how you might adjust or differentiate the tasks in a co-teaching, inclusive classroom.

Student characteristics	Level of difficulty of the task or lesson		What might we do to address the content of this task, considering the student's characteristics?
	Easy	Difficult	
1. Typically achieving student who is on grade level for reading and writing, is motivated, and has good cognitive skills.	1 2 3 4 5		
2. Student who reads very slowly, word by word, has difficulty deciphering unknown words, and skips over long words.	1 2 3 4 5		
3. Student who has difficulty making connections and comprehending reading materials.	1 2 3 4 5		
4. Student who has difficulty with the mechanics of writing, including sentence structure, spelling, and handwriting.	1 2 3 4 5		
5. Student who has difficulty organizing thoughts and information. Written work is very short and incomplete with little idea development.	1 2 3 4 5		
6. Student who is a very concrete thinker. Is able to remember facts, but doesn't understand the big ideas.	1 2 3 4 5		
7. Student who has difficulty processing information when it is given orally, such as through lecturing.	1 2 3 4 5		
8. Student who has difficulty attending to tasks, slow to start work, and often hands in incomplete assignments.	1 2 3 4 5		
9. Student who has difficulty remembering information. Each lesson seems to be a "first" lesson on the topic.	1 2 3 4 5		

Is preparation of materials the responsibility of both co-teachers?

Ideally, analyzing and creating materials is a team effort. In reality, the general education co-teacher often shares a handout or materials with the special education co-teacher who suggests ways of adapting the materials based on anticipated challenges to students. Eventually, scrutinizing materials for the difficulties and the specific challenges experienced by their students becomes integrated into both teachers' framework, and materials become more student friendly.

What elements of design are important when designing materials for diverse learners in a co-taught class?

Co-teachers need not feel that they have to customize every assignment, but an understanding of task demands *is* critical. Following general guidelines of print media is the first step to making materials accessible to the diversity of students in co-taught classes.

- Font size and type
    - 12-point font size allows for ease of reading, although larger type (e.g., 18 point) is appropriate for younger students.
    - A font that is too large restricts students' ability to chunk information.
    - Type should be familiar and easy to read such as Times New Roman.
    - Avoid fanciful fonts; avoid mixing fonts.

- Bold, italics, capitals
    - Overuse of bold letters, italics, or capitals causes students to have difficulty reading the material.

- Text alignment
    - Left-justify typed material to support the eye movement of reading.
    - Center justification disturbs the natural flow of reading.
    - Fully justify text in columns.

- White space
    - Pages should make use of white space to allow students to focus on important information.
    - Avoid packing the page with too much text.

- Printing
  - Although double-sided printing is environmentally recommended, printing on just one side of a page allows students to lay out pages to find answers to questions.

We have a collection of exams that we call the Good, the Bad, and the Ugly simply because of layout and design issues. Co-teachers must make sure that their tests assess knowledge and the format does not interfere with performance. Co-teachers following these general considerations ensure that the grades students receive are more a reflection of what the student knows rather than a result of poorly formatted exams.

- Multiple-choice questions
  - List choices vertically rather than horizontally.
  - Make sure that if the choices are listed as ABCD, the answer sheet corresponds with answers labeled ABCD and not numbers; number choices with number answer sheet.
  - If necessary, allow students to indicate the correct answer on the test instead of transferring to an answer sheet.
  - Insert at least two blank lines between questions.
  - Give three choices instead of the usual four.
  - Highlight key vocabulary or direction words.
  - Allow students to write on test.

- Fill in the blank
  - If necessary, provide a word bank (no more than eight words).

- Matching columns
  - Put the longer descriptions in the first column, with shorter descriptors in the second column. This layout prompts students to read the longer descriptor and then scan the shorter descriptors for the answer, saving time and effort particularly for students with weak reading skills.

- Number of questions
  - The number of questions on some exams may be reduced from an original test, but there needs to be a sufficient number to adequately test learning of the content. A test of 40 items might be reduced to 30 questions that adequately assess the topic.

- Content of questions
  - Determine the most essential information that students must master. The information need not be simply vocabulary or simply require lower-order thinking information. Construct approximately 70 percent of the test using questions from the essential category, allowing co-teachers to feel confident that students who fail the exam lack an understanding of the important elements of the unit. (See Figure 5.1, p. 84.)
  - Construct the remaining 30 percent of the questions to require knowledge of the more intricate or incidental information, or questions that ask for information in a more complicated manner. More specifically, 20 percent of questions should be able to be answered by most students, and 10 percent of questions should be able to be answered by some students.

- Sequencing of questions
  - Scaffold the exam by putting similar questions together, and begin with easier questions and progress to harder questions. Using the Test Assessment Chart (Figure 5.1), insert the number of the test question in the appropriate area on the chart according to the proportion of students who should be able to answer the question (all, most, some) and the level of the question's difficulty (easy, moderate, hard). By doing so, co-teachers can make sure that their test assesses the depth and breadth of material in a fair manner.

In addition to attending to instructional elements and materials, how do co-teachers create an effective classroom environment?

Effective co-teachers understand the role that environment plays in supporting the diversity of learners in the classroom, and they expand the concept of environment to include the physical setup of the classroom, along with curriculum, instructional, and social and emotional environments. Supportive environments emanate from co-teachers, including efficient knowledge and presentation of content in an atmosphere created to ensure the optimal learning of all students. What might be construed as a minor detail can be a major stumbling block to students with special needs. The creation of a supportive co-teaching classroom is facilitated by analyzing all components of the learning environment. Co-teachers can increase their effectiveness when they look critically at the environments they've created, understanding that learning is enhanced through an emphasis on the physical appeal of the classroom, the careful selection of what is to be taught, the knowledge of effective teaching techniques, and the goal of every student's well-being.

Physical environment

Arranging furniture. Particular configurations of desks can support attention and active learning. Arranging the desks in a U shape allows for extended interactions among students and co-teachers, and avoids having students seated in the far back of the class. Another great configuration makes use of multiple U-shape groupings, allowing for easy access to stations and group work.

Posting of routines, special events, and a calendar of assignment due dates. Having the daily schedule posted with pictures or color codes helps students get an overall idea of the day and facilitates easy transitions between activities. Posting calendars with test and project due dates, along with suggestions for pacing study or project tasks, helps students organize their time and work and is particularly effective for those students who have difficulty starting and systematically working on an assignment.

Displaying posters and student work. Although classrooms barren of art and student work products are sterile and unappealing, avoid cluttering the classroom with so many posters, student work examples, storage bins, supplies, and books that the environment is distracting for students.

Curriculum and instructional environments

Prioritizing the curriculum. Today's curriculum and standards can be overwhelming, particularly with the inclination to "cover" everything. Understanding that concentrating on the big ideas of content can help students learn content more thoroughly makes an ever-expanding curriculum manageable.

Using UDL components. Devising lessons that provide for multiple means of representation, engagement, and expression respects the diversity of learners in a co-taught classroom and creates opportunities for students with and without special needs to succeed.

Ensuring student understanding. By carefully analyzing lessons and materials and using co-teaching models that decrease the student-to-teacher ratio, co-teachers continually check student understanding.

Monitoring progress. Intrinsic in a co-taught class is monitoring student understanding and progress. Daily attention to what students are learning and reflecting on co-teaching techniques and lessons lead to adjustments in teaching. Formal monitoring and charting of learning through curriculum-based measurement enables co-teachers to closely watch the effectiveness of their teaching.

Using a variety of co-teaching models. The versatility of using all co-teaching models helps co-teachers to create environments that optimize learning, increase attention and student participation, customize instruction, and monitor learning. By diversifying teaching methods the co-teachers can keep students interested, involved, and engaged.

Teaching and using specific learning strategies. Often teachers think that they are teaching a strategy when they are simply asking students to perform a strategy. For instance, asking students to highlight the important information is useless unless students know how to decipher the important elements in a reading. Co-teachers understand the importance of strategic learning and know that learning strategies must be carefully and intentionally taught, used, and reinforced.

Creating and adapting materials. How materials are formatted and presented to students can make a major difference in their successful completion of the task. An understanding of the needs of students and the positive effects of customized materials helps co-teachers create possibilities of success for students.

Maximizing student engagement. Many students approach learning in a passive manner. Lecture-style lessons can reinforce this passivity. Students learn best when they are actively engaged in lessons and activities. The ability of co-teachers to engage students is enhanced by the ability to break into a variety of groupings.

Social and emotional environments

Addressing and accepting diversity. Classrooms hold students with a wide range of learning differences, as well as cultural, racial, linguistic, and physical differences. The best inclusive co-taught classes openly address differences, similarities, and notions of fairness.

Expecting achievement and success. Although acknowledging the various struggles that students may encounter on their path to learning, the primary goal of a co-taught inclusive class is for each child to learn and succeed. Expectations are high for students as well as for co-teachers; co-teachers who understand how together they can best support struggling students achieve success.

Creating a safe place for risk taking and failure. Students with special needs in co-taught classes face tremendous learning challenges. Although there are high expectations, students will experience some failures and slow progress. All students, especially those with the most challenges, will be motivated to try for success through the support of co-teachers and their careful planning of appropriate lessons and tasks.

Maintaining a safe classroom. By sharing a position on how to manage classroom behaviors, and consistently, fairly, and firmly insisting on adherence to class rules, co-teachers can create a safe learning environment. In addition, co-teachers strive to support and scaffold instruction because they understand that how they orchestrate learning activities directly affects student behavior.

Insisting on an atmosphere of respect and dignity. When differences are acknowledged, understood, and celebrated, and when similarities are highlighted, students and co-teachers create an environment that supports respect for and dignity of each individual. When co-teachers value each other's and each student's strengths and weaknesses, they model the attributes they want from their students.

———————•••———————

Case Study 11

How can we increase student motivation?

TJ has always experienced difficulties in school. Although he is quite smart and interested in anything that has to do with nature, his reading and writing skills are significantly below grade level. TJ seldom does his homework and hands projects in late, if at all. He is always behind in classroom assignments and is expected to finish his work at home if it's not complete in class. He passes tests marginally; his report card grades are passing but poor. The co-teachers don't understand his behavior because they give him credit for attempting homework—and doing part of the projects would significantly enhance his grade. They feel TJ just doesn't care and believe that unless he changes his work habits, TJ will likely fail for the year.

Statement of the problem

Co-teachers are not designing homework that considers student needs.

Problem genesis

TJ has significant deficits in reading and writing skills, making it difficult for him to complete work independently.

How the problem is being denied or addressed

TJ's co-teachers believe that he is unmotivated and uninterested in school. They have not compared TJ's skills and challenges against the demands of the assignments.

Ways of promoting a positive outcome

• TJ's co-teachers need to look at the independent assignments and reflect on the difficulty levels of the assignments and adapt the materials accordingly. Using tools such as the Rating Scale for Teaching Materials (Figure 6.5) and the Task and Lesson Rating Scale (Figure 6.6) will help them guide their assessment of the materials.

• Keeping in mind elements of Universal Design for Learning, the co-teachers can create assignments and materials that are presented in a variety of ways and require responses that will not tax TJ's skills. For instance, TJ could create a PowerPoint presentation instead of a traditional book report.

• The co-teachers could involve TJ in conversations regarding modifications and changes in assignments to help him understand and overtly appreciate that the arrangements are geared toward his success.

• Graphing TJ's homework and project performance would give TJ a concrete way of seeing and monitoring his progress.

• Specifically working on TJ's IEP reading and writing goals would help to improve his performance. The co-teachers need to incorporate strategies that specifically target reading recognition, comprehension, and written expression. Homogeneous groupings through an alternate model several times a week might help address the IEP goals.

Case Study 12

How can we increase student performance on exams?

Ms. Vivasi and Ms. Ellenworth co-teach a 4th grade inclusive class. Many students, including those with special needs, are doing poorly on science exams. The curriculum is interesting, though somewhat difficult. Although the class curriculum includes many experiments, the students do not generalize what they learn to questions on tests. The students are easily confused, but the co-teachers don't want to water down the curriculum or the tests. They give students study guides the night before the tests and homework on the material each night. The co-teachers are frustrated and feel that maybe the skill levels of the students with special needs are too low and other students are just not putting in enough time or effort.

Statement of the problem

Many students are not learning the science curriculum well enough to perform at a sufficient level on the exams.

Problem genesis

The science curriculum is extensive, and many of the students have poor skills.

How the problem is being denied or addressed

The co-teachers are teaching the content but leaving the responsibility for how to learn to the students.

Ways of promoting a positive outcome

• The co-teachers should review the science tests and make sure that the tests are student-friendly and formatted for ease of completion. The exams can also be minimally adapted by highlighting the important parts of the questions.

• The co-teachers should incorporate effective instruction practices during each lesson, particularly focusing on similarities and differences and summarizing information to reinforce the important information and bring understanding to a higher level.

• Review sheets could be incorporated throughout the units so that students have time to review the important information (not just the night before the test).

• At the end of each day's lesson, ask students to respond to the content in a way that allows the co-teachers to assess what was learned, what was confusing, and what needs to be retaught or reinforced.

• The co-teachers should make sure that content is taught using multiple approaches and capitalize on their ability to teach in small groupings.

It's pretty hard to work on skills and give students the strategies that they need. My co-teacher and I are always talking about our students and thinking about how to improve their skills. We've decided to incorporate a few basic strategies for writing and reading into our daily plans, teach them to all the students, and demonstrate how using the strategies will improve their work.

—High school special education co-teacher

My special education co-teacher has really helped me to understand how I need to focus on skills and content. I've used a lot of the learning and teaching strategies in the classes that I teach by myself. I can see how they can help most students.

—Middle school general education co-teacher

We are excited about how all our students are doing on tests and exams. We decided that our students needed to review more, but we couldn't count on them studying at home. We now review regularly. In fact, we make sure that we do some review games at least once a week and we also put students in small groups to do quick reviews at the end of most of our lessons. It has really made a difference. We (and our students) couldn't be happier with the results.

—Elementary co-teachers

7

Incorporating Teaching Strategies

Mr. Bowker can't believe his co-teacher talked him into participating in the Strategy Rap! Mr. Gioia loves music and Mr. Bowker thinks it's great that music is part of the class. But rapping in class? Mr. Gioia made up a rap on the strategies they were going to use in this unit, and now Mr. Bowker and Mr. Gioia are in front of the class, rapping! Both first-year teachers, Mr. Bowker reflects on how great a year it's been. Both involved in setting up the curriculum from the start, they spent many hours planning what to teach and how to teach it. Mr. Bowker is thankful that he took a co-teaching course as part of his master's in special education. He learned many strategies and different ways of grouping students. As a certified social studies teacher, Mr. Bowker understands the curriculum. He knows that working with another teacher could be difficult and is happy to be having a great co-teaching experience. He hopes that they can continue co-teaching next year but knows there are frequent changes in co-teaching partners.

Mr. Gioia and Mr. Bowker stand in the front of class, taking turns rapping. Mr. Gioia likes to begin each unit with a rap that lets the students know what they are going to learn. Today they are doing a Strategy Rap, outlining the steps to successful paraphrasing and organization of information. Mr. Gioia thinks about the year and how great it's been to teach with Mr. Bowker. Mr. Gioia was somewhat apprehensive when he was told that he would have two inclusion classes and would have to teach with a co-teacher. Having taken only one special education course and being a first-year teacher, Mr. Gioia didn't know how he was going to create lessons and meet the needs of all the students in the class. Looking back on the year with Mr. Bowker, Mr. Gioia is proud of the collaboration and the learning that took place in their co-taught classes.

Strategy Rap

My name is Mr. B and I got some tools
Some learning strategies that can be used in your schools
They are functional, helpful, and oh so easy
You'll so fly through the Regents it'll make you queasy

My name is Mr. G and I'm here to say
I got some educational strategies to put on your tray
First let's talk about RAP
It's like writing yourself a reading map

First step to take is start to read
The next two steps will help you succeed
Next you gotta ask yourself who or what it's about
This is the step you can't do without
Lastly you gotta put it in your own words
This strategy can even help the nerds

Next we got the BCF plan
Easy enough for a cave man
First, just write the topic in the middle
This is not a test or a riddle
Draw four boxes around the center
This gives you space for information to enter
We have given you the tools to succeed
These strategies will help keep you up to speed
Doing well on the Regents is your new task
If you have any questions don't hesitate to ask.

—© 2010 Justin Gioia and Dan Bowker. Printed with permission.

What are the best strategies for helping both general education students and students with special needs in a co-taught class?

Research and evidenced-based practices are widely promoted in an effort to improve the effectiveness of instruction in every classroom. Increasingly, the programs and strategies deemed successful are adopted by educators—with more or less success. Researchers often point to variations in the generalizability of findings to differences in populations and the fidelity with which practitioners implement the practice. Ultimately, the *best* practice or strategy is one that is working in a particular classroom for specific students. Co-teachers who are reflective and monitor student progress continually assess what is working and how much students are learning. To successfully provide special education services within the inclusive classroom and to provide access to the standard curriculum, co-teachers must intentionally and intensively address the needs of diverse learners.

Strategies abound, but those in this chapter are tried and true, teacher-friendly strategies that correspond to the essential elements of instructional design. As we discussed in Chapter 6, those elements are big ideas, primed background knowledge, conspicuous strategies, mediated scaffolding, and judicious review.

What strategies can co-teachers use to help students learn the big ideas?

Big ideas emphasize those elements of a curriculum that are essential for understanding both the overarching ideas and the specifics within topics. The following strategies help focus teaching and learning on big ideas.

The Basic Concept Format and the **Expanded Concept Format** (Wilson, 2007) create a framework for students to understand both the overriding concept and the important details that contribute to the big ideas. The formats are used for both concepts and content. Many students need the big ideas matched with specific information to understand the material and transform this knowledge into higher-order thinking, writing, and discussions. These formats give students a structure to collect information in a manner that promotes understanding and remembering. Steps to creating a Basic Concept Format (BCF):

1. Divide a square into four segments with a circle in the center.

2. Insert the concept into the center circle.

3. Discuss as a group (or the teacher can supply) the basic elements of the concept. The four headers are the big ideas that are needed to deeply understand the concept and are prototypical. For instance, as depicted in Figure 7.1, if exploration is the concept, the four headers might be (1) countries and explorers, (2) colonies, (3) reasons, and (4) effects (Figure 7.1). These headers might be applicable for each exploration topic students study (e.g., European Exploration of the New World; European Exploration of Africa).

The Expanded Concept Format (ECF) further delineates the information from the BCF by taking one or all of the defining elements and creating additional frameworks. For instance, a BCF on European Exploration of the New World would lead to an ECF on Colonies with the following headers: (1) where (area of the New World), (2) when, (3) who, and (4) significance. A complete ECF on the colony of Jamestown, shown as Figure 7.2, could be compared with an ECF on the colony of Plymouth or Quebec or New Amsterdam.

When to use in a co-taught setting: The formats are useful in a variety of content areas. Using a parallel model, each co-teacher can develop an expanded concept format (for instance, colonization of the new world), then bring the class together to compare and contrast how different countries colonized North America. The format can be used whenever important concepts or vocabulary need to be learned. Using a station model, the co-teachers can set up an independent station where students work individually, in pairs, or in a group to investigate the concepts or vocabulary words.

The Framing Routine

The Framing Routine is a powerful strategy used to organize key concepts, define details, and support a thesis statement. Developed by Ellis (2008, p. 53), Frames help students organize and develop big ideas and create an organization and structure for a thesis statement defense. Steps in the Framing Routine:

1. Focus student attention on the topic.
2. Reveal the main ideas that will be explored and how they are related.
3. Analyze and record the most significant details of each main idea.
4. Make a statement that helps students understand the lesson within a larger context—a "so what" statement.
5. Extend understanding of the information.

Figure 7.1 | Basic Concept Format

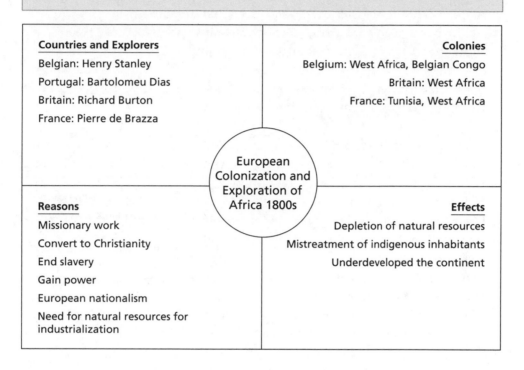

Countries and Explorers
Belgian: Henry Stanley
Portugal: Bartolomeu Dias
Britain: Richard Burton
France: Pierre de Brazza

Colonies
Belgium: West Africa, Belgian Congo
Britain: West Africa
France: Tunisia, West Africa

European Colonization and Exploration of Africa 1800s

Reasons
Missionary work
Convert to Christianity
End slavery
Gain power
European nationalism
Need for natural resources for industrialization

Effects
Depletion of natural resources
Mistreatment of indigenous inhabitants
Underdeveloped the continent

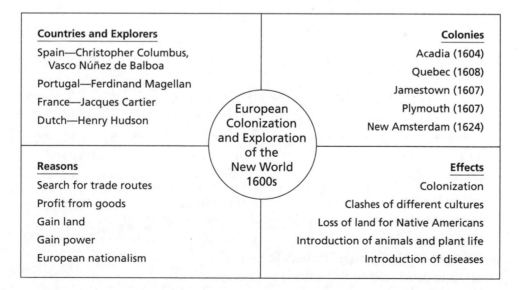

Countries and Explorers
Spain—Christopher Columbus, Vasco Núñez de Balboa
Portugal—Ferdinand Magellan
France—Jacques Cartier
Dutch—Henry Hudson

Colonies
Acadia (1604)
Quebec (1608)
Jamestown (1607)
Plymouth (1607)
New Amsterdam (1624)

European Colonization and Exploration of the New World 1600s

Reasons
Search for trade routes
Profit from goods
Gain land
Gain power
European nationalism

Effects
Colonization
Clashes of different cultures
Loss of land for Native Americans
Introduction of animals and plant life
Introduction of diseases

Figure 7.2 | **Expanded Concept Format**

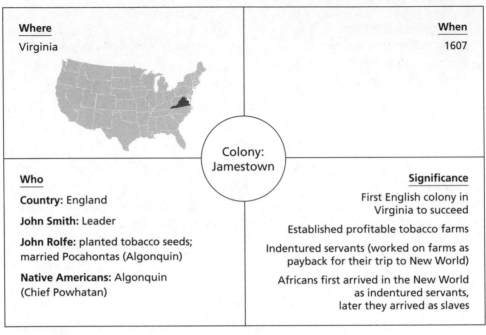

Where
Virginia

When
1607

Colony:
Jamestown

Who

Country: England

John Smith: Leader

John Rolfe: planted tobacco seeds; married Pocahontas (Algonquin)

Native Americans: Algonquin (Chief Powhatan)

Significance

First English colony in Virginia to succeed

Established profitable tobacco farms

Indentured servants (worked on farms as payback for their trip to New World)

Africans first arrived in the New World as indentured servants, later they arrived as slaves

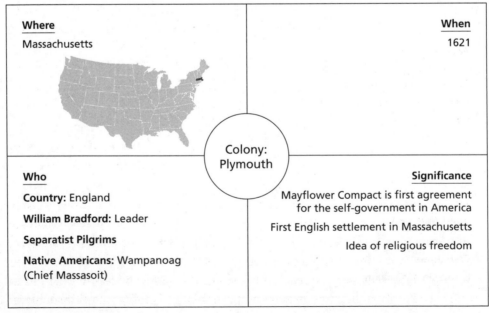

Where
Massachusetts

When
1621

Colony:
Plymouth

Who

Country: England

William Bradford: Leader

Separatist Pilgrims

Native Americans: Wampanoag (Chief Massasoit)

Significance

Mayflower Compact is first agreement for the self-government in America

First English settlement in Massachusetts

Idea of religious freedom

The frame itself is a graphic organizer and is used to guide thinking. The first section is a large rectangular box for the introduction and thesis statement; below the introduction box are three horizontal boxes for the three main ideas that frame the thesis statement. Below each main idea box are additional boxes for the details that support it. Finally, a conclusion or "so what" box spreads across the bottom of the page to provide space for the students to relate the topic to a larger context.

When to use in a co-taught setting: The Framing Routine can be used as a thinking organizer before writing and as a guide to writing. It offers a structure for students to use in developing and organizing their thoughts on a topic. Once the organizer is complete, students can use it as a study guide, a guide for writing powerful essays, or as a guide for informed in-depth discussions. Co-teachers can scaffold the use of Frames, if needed. For instance, both co-teachers could work with two or three students at a time to discuss the main ideas and details of an essay topic and to fill out a Frames organizer. The rest of the class can be working independently on their own organizers and essays.

Concept Mastery Routine

Students and teachers can use the Concept Mastery Routine (Lenz, Deshler, & Kissam, 2004) to investigate ideas by discussing characteristics that are always, sometimes, or never present using examples and nonexamples. The investigation allows students to focus on the many components of a concept and helps them to thoroughly understand the concept as well as to make informed choices on multiple-choice questions. Steps to creating a concept mastery template:

1. Create a template by titling a page with the concept.
2. Below the title, draw three horizontal boxes with labels: Always, Sometimes, and Never.
3. Below those boxes, create two additional horizontal boxes with labels: Examples and Nonexamples.

When to use in a co-taught setting: Concept Mastery is extremely useful when a thorough investigation of a complex overarching concept (e.g., mammals) is needed. The process is difficult, particularly differentiating between the Always, Sometimes, and Never categories, but can be used to great effect in a parallel model where co-teachers develop the same concept with different groups. The groups then merge and compare their development of the concept.

What strategies can co-teachers use to help students activate and develop background knowledge?

Priming background knowledge requires co-teachers to connect what is being learned to students' experiences or former learning, and accentuates the need to teach the foundation for understanding the curriculum. Showing You-Tube segments is a fabulous way to activate student knowledge on a particular topic. Here are other strategies to help prime students' knowledge to gain understanding of an upcoming topic.

Anticipation Guides

Anticipation guides (Kozen, Murray, & Windell, 2006) contain a list of statements that are related to the topic the students will be studying. Students indicate whether they agree or disagree with declarative statements before the topic is studied and again after the unit or lesson. These guides activate students' prior knowledge, enhance comprehension, and build interest. Used to provide a means for teachers to assess student knowledge, Anticipation Guides also serve as thinking tools when a topic is introduced and as a way to reflect on original ideas at the end of a topic. To create an Anticipation Guide (Figure 7.3):

1. The teacher chooses five or six declarative statements that address the essential components of the topic to be taught, whether factual or common misconceptions.

2. The teacher or the students write the statements on a graphic organizer that allows space before and after each statement (narrow columns suitable for Yes/No or Agree/Disagree responses by each student).

3. As a group or individually, students decide whether they agree with each statement and circle their best answer.

4. Discussion can follow as to why students answered as they did. The Anticipation Guide is again referenced at the end of the topic, and students can discuss how their answers stayed the same or changed as they learned more about the topic.

When to use in a co-taught setting: Anticipation Guides can be used at the beginning of a reading assignment or unit to evaluate what students know and how they feel about a topic. After the lessons, the Anticipation Guide can help teachers evaluate how well students understand the material and to correct misconceptions. In a teaming model, the co-teachers can supply different opinions on each statement.

Figure 7.3	**Anticipation Guide**

Anticipation Guide: Colonial America					
Before the Unit			**Statements**	**After the Unit**	
Agree	**Disagree**	**Not Sure**	All colonists came to the New World for religious freedom.	**Agree**	**Disagree**
Agree	**Disagree**	**Not Sure**	Colonists from England were hardworking and believed in education.	**Agree**	**Disagree**
Agree	**Disagree**	**Not Sure**	There were slaves in the early colonies.	**Agree**	**Disagree**
Agree	**Disagree**	**Not Sure**	Women were among the first settlers.	**Agree**	**Disagree**
Agree	**Disagree**	**Not Sure**	The Native Americans and the colonists were friendly with each other.	**Agree**	**Disagree**

Alphabet Taxonomy

Using this strategy, students list the letters of the alphabet and associate words that begin with each letter with the topic that will be taught. Alphabet Taxonomy (Rothstein, Rothstein & Lauber, 2006) helps those students who have difficulties retrieving information or connecting what they know to what they will be learning. A letter stimulus often helps students to remember what they know about the topic. Used to assess prior knowledge, the Alphabet Taxonomy allows co-teachers to evaluate what students already know about a topic and to discover possible misconceptions. Having this knowledge assists planning. Guide your students in creating an Alphabet Taxonomy:

1. Write the topic at the top of the page.
2. List the letters of the alphabet vertically, on the left side of the paper.
3. Insert words or phrases about the topic corresponding to the letter of the alphabet that it starts with.

When to use in a co-taught setting: A think-pair-share technique works well with Alphabet Taxonomy. Working in parallel groups, the co-teachers give directions and allow students about two minutes to fill in as much as they can. Then, the students pair up to see if they can come up with more details. Students are given an opportunity to share some of their ideas with the small group; finally, the groups merge and combine their lists for a single class list. The information on the original Alphabet Taxonomy that was done at the start of a topic can also be expanded by adding vocabulary that is learned as the unit is taught and used as a reference for review.

What conspicuous strategies can co-teachers teach students to assist learning?

Conspicuous strategies consider the learning efficiency of students. As co-teachers plan instruction, they can enhance successful learning when they show the strategy (make it conspicuous to students) and teach it in stages from modeling, to independent practice, through generalization of use.

The Strategic Instruction Model

The Strategic Instruction Model (SIM), from the University of Kansas, is a series of teaching and learning routines and strategies specifically designed to support content learning. A brief description of four of the basic SIM learning strategies follow: RAP, DISSECT, INFERENCE, and LINCS. Please note that the learning strategies are meant to be taught to students using a precise teaching framework developed at the university, and success is hinged on correct implementation.

RAP (Schumaker, Denton, & Deshler, 1984) is an inferencing strategy designed to increase awareness of pertinent information in a paragraph by paraphrasing the main idea and two supporting details. Students learn how to ask themselves questions as they read and monitor their understanding. The RAP strategy is used paragraph by paragraph, and at times even sentence by sentence for an entire passage, chapter, or page.

RAP, a seemingly simple strategy, provides students with a powerful tool to understand the material that they read because differentiating between what is important and incidental is often difficult. The RAP strategy increases reading comprehension, as well as paraphrasing skills, and enables students to capture the big ideas as well as details. The steps students use for RAP:

1. Read the paragraph
2. Ask questions about the main idea and details
3. Put the information in their own words

When to use in a co-taught setting: RAP can be used in class while reading a difficult text, paragraph by paragraph, or even sentence by sentence. It can be done one-on-one with a co-teacher, in alternate groups, in small groups with partners, or individually. RAP can also be used with a homework assignment or to monitor students' progress and understanding of the material.

DISSECT (Lenz, Schumaker, Deshler, & Beals, 1984) is a word identification strategy used by older students to decipher unknown words. Students with reading difficulties often have trouble with word recognition, word retrieval, and decoding. Breaking words into syllables through DISSECT is a systematic process that helps students read and understand unknown words. Students use the method when they are reading a passage with multisyllabic words and discover an unfamiliar word:

*   Discover the context.
*   Isolate the prefix.
*   Separate the suffix.
*   Say the stem.
*   Examine the stem.
*   Check with someone.
*   Try the dictionary (p. 95).

When to use in a co-taught setting: DISSECT should be used by students who already have basic reading skills. Used while reading a passage, or after, to help better understand what is read, DISSECT gives older students a method to decipher unknown words. DISSECT is easily integrated into any co-teaching model when students are reading.

Inference (Fritschmann, Deshler, & Schumaker, 2007, Cue card 14) is a comprehension strategy that helps students successfully answer questions after reading passages. Inference trains students to recognize different types of questions, whether they are factual questions or "think and seek" questions (big picture, predicting, and clarifying). Many students struggle tremendously with comprehension and higher-order skills, such as making inferences. Research results show that students who learned the inference strategy improved their ability to make inferences and to identify different types of questions. Students performed significantly better on tests, including standardized reading assessments, after learning this strategy, which focuses on making students more active and strategic learners. Students INFER when they

- Interact with the questions in the passage by previewing the material and questions, and dividing the questions into two categories: Factual or Think and Seek.
- Categorize the Think and Seek questions into big picture, predicting, and clarifying questions.
- Note what they know by activating background knowledge or experiences that are related to the topic.
- Find the clues by reading the passage and underlining clues that are directly related to the question.
- Explore supporting details by looking for details that enhance the tentative answer.
- Return to the question and check that an answer has been selected or recorded.
- Discuss the answers.

When to use in a co-taught setting: Inference may be used during or after any reading comprehension passage that has questions to be answered. The strategy works well in a station model where each co-teacher directs a group focusing on one type of question and students in the independent group come up with their own questions using the types of questions learned in inference.

LINCS vocabulary strategy (Ellis, 2003) is a vocabulary strategy that promotes learning of content vocabulary that is particularly challenging for students. LINCS entails creating note cards with segmented boxes labeled *Word, Reminding words, Definition, Reminding sentence, Reminding picture* and following a series of steps. The LINCS strategy helps students learn the meaning of unknown vocabulary words using powerful memory-enhancement techniques. The strategy steps cue students to focus on critical elements of the word, use visual cues or imagery, and make some associations with prior knowledge. Here are the steps to using LINCS:

1. List the parts: The students are given or make a note card that has the vocabulary word and definition, plus sections for reminding words, reminding sentence, and reminding picture.

2. Identify reminding words: The students come up with words found within the vocabulary word or that closely rhyme with a part of the word.

3. Note a LINCing story: Students create a sentence that includes the definition and the reminding word (not the vocabulary word).

4. Create a LINCing picture: Students draw a picture that depicts the reminding sentence.

5. Self-test.

When to use in a co-taught setting: LINCS can be used by groups, in pairs of students, or individually, and it is particularly suitable to an independent station. It can be used in many subjects including English, social studies, and science. A complete set of LINCS note cards is effectively used as a study guide for vocabulary tests. Some teachers provide photo albums for students to arrange their LINCS cards.

Peer-Assisted Learning Strategies

Peer-Assisted Learning Strategies (PALS) are a series of strategies, including Retell and Paragraph Shrinking developed by researchers at Vanderbilt University. High-achieving students are paired with lower-achieving peers and go through specific steps to increase reading and math skills.

Retell is a strategy used by students working in pairs. They take turns listening and retelling the main ideas of what is read. Retell (Master, 2006) is a strategy that pinpoints the important parts of a passage, a skill that is often difficult for many students. The student pairs must pay close attention to what is read in order to agree on the retelling of the story. After co-teachers select the reading passages and carefully assign students to pairs:

1. Each partner reads for a maximum of 5 minutes.

2. The partner who is listening prompts: What happened first? What happened next? What's the main idea?

3. If either partner disagrees with the summary, they discuss the dissension before moving on.

4. Co-teachers monitor progress of the pairs.

When to use in a co-taught setting: Retell is used in pairs during class to improve reading comprehension and fluency. Using a parallel model, co-teachers can moderate the work of the students and periodically lead a discussion within the groups about the reading.

Paragraph Shrinking is similar to RAP in that it is an activity for pairs of students who take turns reading and summarizing the main points of each paragraph. Students provide one another with feedback as a way to check comprehension. Paragraph Shrinking (Fuchs, Fuchs, & Burish, 2000) provides students with a powerful way to delineate the main ideas of passages, a skill many students find difficult. After selecting a reading passage and assigning students to pairs:

1. Each student reads aloud to a partner without rereading the text.
2. After each paragraph, the students stop to summarize the main points.
3. Students decide who or what each paragraph is about, and what is important about the who or what.
4. If the students disagree, they silently skim the paragraph again and answer the question a second time.
5. Students switch reading and listening tasks.
6. Progress is monitored and checked for correct responses.

When to use in a co-taught setting: Paragraph Shrinking is recommended for intervals of between 25 and 40 minutes and is used to improve reading comprehension skills. Once the students are familiar with the strategy, it fits well into a station model as an independent group.

How can co-teachers use mediated scaffolding to enhance learning?

Mediated scaffolding addresses the needs of some students with learning difficulties to be guided to higher levels of thinking and understanding. A properly scaffolded lesson enables students to demonstrate cognitive strengths. Co-teachers include mediated scaffolding strategies in their lesson structures and frameworks to assist students in the acquisition and synthesis of curriculum and to gradually support independent learning.

I-Format

The I-Format is a graphic organizer that enables teachers to arrange information in a simple but comprehensive manner. The I-Format is made up of two horizontal rectangular boxes joined by a long vertical rectangular box (forming a capital *I*). The I-Format contains vocabulary, rationale, steps, and examples.

This graphic organizer is often used to compile series of information, such as math logarithms, so that students can see and use the multiple components to compare and contrast among topics or as a model for independent work. Steps to designing an I-Format for adding decimals:

1. At the top center of the first horizontal box put the topic or title (i.e., How to Add Decimals).
2. Under the title, insert vocabulary and definitions, along with an explanation about why students need to know the topic.
3. In the vertical box that forms the trunk of the *I*, put the steps for adding decimals.
4. In the bottom horizontal box, insert examples of how to add decimals.

When to use in a co-taught model: Whenever you have a series of topics that can be presented in a similar fashion, the I-Format is an appropriate organizer. For instance, when used in math, the headings in the first box could be Vocabulary and Why Are We Learning This. Put steps in the vertical box and insert examples (from easy to hard) into the bottom rectangle. Used in a teaming model or one teach, one support, the I-Format can be completed as a minilesson taught to the entire class, and then used when the class moves into parallel groups for guided practice or discussion.

Math Frame

The Math Frame is a graphic organizer that helps students scaffold information in applied math problems (word problems). Many students have difficulties applying their computation skills to word problems, so the Math Frame format helps them organize information as shown in Figure 7.4. Scaffolding the information into sections helps students learn how to systematically solve the problems. After reading the word problem in the top box, students follow these steps:

1. Insert the information given.
2. Record the information needed.
3. Explain the steps to be used to solve the problem (how).
4. Do the work required by the problem.
5. Write the answer under the box that described what information was needed.

Figure 7.4 | Multiple-Step Math Frame

In 1621, 102 colonists landed in Plymouth; 49 died before the first Thanksgiving. If only 4 women were at the first Thanksgiving, how many attendees were men?

Information Given	Information Needed	How	Work
• 102 colonists landed • 4 were women • 49 died before the first Thanksgiving	How many colonists were at the first Thanksgiving?	Subtract how many died from how many landed.	102 colonists −49 died 53 colonists at Thanksgiving
	Information Needed How many men celebrated the first Thanksgiving?	**How** Subtract the number of women from the number of people who celebrated Thanksgiving.	**Work** colonists at 53 Thanksgiving −4 women 49 men
	Answer 49 men were at the first Thanksgiving.		

For multistep word problems, divide the organizer so each step shows the information needed, strategy (how), and work.

When to use in a co-taught setting: The Math Frame can be used whenever word problems are assigned to students and may be completed with the assistance of a teacher or partner. The teacher may scaffold students' work by partially filling in the organizer when the process is new and, as students become more familiar with the process, provide fewer answers. When intensive support is needed, the Math Frame can be used in an alternate co-teaching model setting.

Adapted Venn diagram

Venn diagrams are intersecting circles that display common and unique attributes of two or more topics or ideas. The Adapted Venn diagram (see the example in Figure 7.5), adds a series of horizontal lines that start to the left of the first circle and run straight through the two circles to the right side of the diagram. Traditional Venn diagrams assume that students will mentally categorize information and then make a decision as to whether the particular attribute is unique or shared, and insert it appropriately within the diagram. Many students with learning difficulties, however, have trouble categorizing information. In the adapted version, the teacher can provide the categories on the lines that are outside the circle. The student then gives an answer related to the category, compares and contrasts the concept based on the category, and places the attribute appropriately. Here's how to create an Adapted Venn diagram:

1. Draw two intersecting circles on a piece of paper.
2. Draw horizontal lines that begin at the left margin of the paper and intersect the circles.
3. Write general categories of attributes to be considered on the lines outside the circles (the teacher or student may provide the categories and attributes or answers).
4. Ask the student to insert the specific attribute related to the category into the proper place in the circles, depending on whether the attribute is unique or shared.

Figure 7.5 | Adapted Venn Diagram

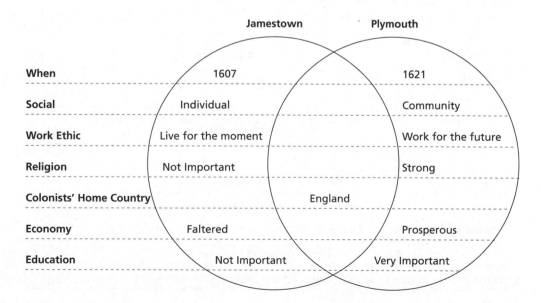

	Jamestown		Plymouth
When	1607		1621
Social	Individual		Community
Work Ethic	Live for the moment		Work for the future
Religion	Not Important		Strong
Colonists' Home Country		England	
Economy	Faltered		Prosperous
Education	Not Important		Very Important

When to use in a co-taught setting: The Adapted Venn diagram can be used whenever students need to compare and contrast information. Used in a station model, the Adapted Venn can be an independent or guided station.

Questioning Taxonomy

The Questioning Taxonomy (Buehl, 2009) is a framework for student or teacher-generated questions. This strategy features questioning prompts built on basic facts and on Bloom's taxonomy: remembering, understanding, applying, analyzing, evaluating, and creating. Using this strategy, teachers can scaffold information to raise basic and deep questions. Inspection of student-generated questions can assist teachers in accessing student understanding of the material. Students or teachers use the Questioning Taxonomy to generate appropriate questions at different levels after reading a text or completing a unit. The questions are listed in a hierarchy, as shown in Figure 7.6.

When to use in a co-taught setting: The Questioning Taxonomy can be used at the end of a lesson or unit, after reading selected passages, and for homework. In a parallel model, co-teachers can decide to use all or some of the questions to hold discussions.

Figure 7.6 | Questioning Taxonomy

Type of Question	Sample Questions
Yes/No	Were both Jamestown and Plymouth early colonies established by the English?
Embedded	Did indentured servants pay for their passage from Europe by paying money or working in the New World?
One Word	Where was Jamestown?
List	What three factors helped Jamestown grow?
Elicit	What hardships did the early colonists encounter?
Analysis	How did religion contribute to the growth of Plymouth?
Synthesis	What made Plymouth different from Jamestown?
Evaluation	Why did Plymouth continue to prosper as Jamestown declined?

What techniques can co-teachers implement to carry out judicious review?

Judicious review acknowledges the memory deficits of many students with learning difficulties. Instead of bemoaning the fact that students don't remember or spend enough time studying, co-teachers incorporate memory strategies and repetition as integral parts of instruction.

Peer tutoring

Although there are many variations of peer-assisted learning, commonalities include frequent peer-to-peer interaction and immediate feedback. The peer tutoring organizer comprises questions, answers, and a scoring column. Many students need reinforcement of information in order to retain the material. Peer tutoring offers a simple and student-friendly vehicle to provide opportunities to review and retain information. To create a peer tutoring organizer and session, the teacher follows these steps:

1. Determines the important facts that students need to know for the unit.
2. Starts with the answer column (see Figure 7.7) and inserts one-word answers. The answers cannot be complicated because a peer tutor will score the work. If the tutor doesn't know enough about the question, then he or she can't accurately rate the tutee.
3. Provides the questions. The questions may be complicated.
4. Divides the class into pairs without worrying about ability levels. The students must be able to read the organizer but do not need to know the answers. The tutor gets the complete organizer, which has both the questions and the answers. If the tutees need a visual, a copy of the questions is supplied, and the tutees read along as they listen to tutors pose the questions.
5. The tutor, at the designated time, begins asking the tutee questions.
6. If the tutee answers correctly, the tutor circles the first "C" for Correct.
7. If the tutee responds incorrectly, the tutor circles the first "I" for Incorrect, but the tutor immediately supplies the answer and again asks the question. The tutee now has another chance of getting the correct answer. If the tutee answers correctly this time, the tutor circles the second "C." If the tutee answers incorrectly for the second time, the second "I" is circled. The tutor repeats the correct answer, then asks the next question, and continues until all questions are completed. Students can then switch roles with the same or different questions.

8. If desired, the peer tutoring forms could show a point system instead of Correct/Incorrect.

When to use in a co-taught setting: Many peer tutoring procedures require an extended and frequent time period for peer interactions. For the peer tutoring session, we've found it best to limit the number of questions to 10 and allow between 5 and 7 minutes for the activity. If done twice a week (e.g., Tuesday and Thursday) in place of a Do Now activity, the review process is successful. Students take turns being the tutor or the tutee. One is the tutor on Tuesday, the other is the tutor on Thursday. Co-teachers can also use a parallel model and begin the class by having one group participate in peer tutoring while the other group is reviewing homework.

Figure 7.7 | Peer Tutoring Organizer

Tutee Name: _____   Date: _____

Tutor Name: _____   Time: _____

Question	Answer	Correct/Incorrect	
What was the first agreement for self-government in America?	Mayflower Compact	C I	C I
Who helped found and govern Jamestown?	John Smith	C I	C I
What is a crop that is grown for profit?	Cash crop	C I	C I
Who came to America to work for a period of time to pay for their voyage from Europe?	Indentured servants	C I	C I
What was the first group of elected representatives of English colonists in North America called?	House of Burgesses	C I	C I
Who were a group of English Protestants that worked for religious and societal reforms?	Puritans	C I	C I
What was the tribe of Native Americans that the colonists from Jamestown encountered called?	Powhatan	C I	C I
What was the first settlement in Virginia?	Jamestown	C I	C I
What was the first settlement in Massachusetts?	Plymouth	C I	C I

Response cards with quick drills

Response cards can be any medium on which a student can write the answer to a question—dry-erase boards work well. Quick drills are a selection of questions that are presented to the students to answer in a quick and nonthreatening manner. Response Cards with Quick Drills (Davis & O'Neil, 2004) offer a vehicle for teachers to increase class participation, find time for reinforcement, and assess student knowledge. The bank of questions is cumulative, so all the units learned are represented and frequently and consistently retrieved and assessed. Here's the process for Response Cards with Quick Drills:

1. Select 10 of the most important concepts, vocabulary, and facts from each unit as you teach it.

2. Designate a distinct color of construction paper for each unit (i.e., yellow for unit 1; blue for unit 2), and put each question on a single sheet of construction paper.

3. Shuffle and select five to eight question sheets (picking from each unit or color) to display, and read to the class, one at a time.

4. Ask students to write responses on dry-erase boards and hold up for the co-teachers to view. Students can put a question mark on the board if they do not know the answer.

5. Look at the responses and mentally note who has incorrect answers.

6. One co-teacher, even if there are some students who do not have the correct answer, says, "Yes, the formula for the Pythagorean theorem is $a^2 + b^2 = c^2$."

Note: Make inexpensive dry-erase boards out of sheet protectors with card stock inside. Or, students can simply fold a piece of notebook paper into four horizontal sections and put an answer in each section (there will be a total of eight sections if the back and the front of the paper are used). The papers can be collected, if desired.

When to use in a co-taught setting: Use the Response Cards with Quick Drills twice a week. The strategy can be used in homogeneously grouped stations, with the Quick Drills geared for the level of the group.

Case Study 13

How can we improve written work that is disorganized?

Melique is an 8th grader who has difficulties with organizing her thoughts and expressing them in writing. She easily completes a web of facts on the writing topic, but when she tries to put the facts into an essay, the writing lacks cohesiveness and clarity. Melique unloads all the information that she knows and seems to hope that her teachers will see that she knows the material. Her writing lacks focus and rambles through the facts. Melique's co-teachers usually hold a writing conference with her about each writing sample and then she edits her work. The co-teachers are concerned because Melique's writing skills don't seem to be improving. Her grades in English are negatively affected, and she is also getting poor grades on social studies essays.

Statement of the problem

Melique's co-teachers are at a loss as to how to improve her writing skills.

Problem genesis

The co-teachers continue to use a one-size-fits-all editing strategy that is not improving Melique's writing skills.

How the problem is being denied or addressed

Although conferencing with students and editing their work with them is common to the writing process, Melique's co-teachers are beginning to realize that they need to try a different strategy to address her writing difficulties.

Ways of promoting a positive outcome

• A generic organization format outlining what should be contained in each part of the essay (introduction with thesis statement, three paragraphs of support, and conclusion) may help Melique set up her thoughts before she writes. The organizer may be a guide that Melique can read and follow as she organizes her work or may be graphically represented using the Frames template.

• Co-teachers may scaffold writing by giving Melique a model essay that is cut up into sentences and ask her to put the sentences into the correct order. If Melique has difficulty with this activity, the co-teachers could try again, using a different essay and putting some of the sentences in the correct place. Melique would then fill in the remaining sentences and complete the essay.

• Using Frames, Melique may work through a series of activities to organize the supporting details under the main ideas. For example, if the main idea is supplied, she could insert the details in the appropriate boxes. Alternatively, teachers may supply the details and ask Melique to supply the main ideas.

Case Study 14

How can we improve performance on exams?

Josh is a hardworking 10th grader who does well enough on his social studies quizzes, in part because he studies exactly what is on the study guides that he gets from the co-teachers. When it comes to unit tests, despite the fact that he studies and goes to extra help sessions, he just can't seem to connect information that he knows to the way the questions are asked, and he gets easily confused. His co-teachers are stumped because Josh works so hard and seems to understand the material during class time. He participates and contributes to class discussions and always completes his homework.

Statement of the problem

Despite effort, Josh does poorly on unit tests in social studies.

Problem genesis

Although Josh's reading skills are almost on grade level, he has difficulties interpreting multiple-choice questions. He often can't generalize knowledge to new situations and gets easily confused. He misinterprets essay questions and only partially answers the questions.

How the problem is being denied or addressed

Josh's teachers realize that there is a difference in his performance in class, on quizzes, and on unit tests. Other than encouraging him to come to extra help sessions and continue studying, they don't know what else to do.

Ways of promoting a positive outcome

• The co-teachers need to make sure Josh actually understands not only the facts but the social studies concepts being taught. Memorizing information might be fine for Josh for the short term and contribute to his success on short quizzes, but a thorough understanding of the big ideas should help his performance. Using strategies such as the Basic and Expanded Concept Formats may help integrate details and concepts.

• Josh's teachers could do an error analysis of his answers on multiple-choice questions. By analyzing if his answers are correct, close, or clueless, they can see how far off Josh is in his understanding and interpreting of questions. The Concept Mastery would help Josh get a good understanding of what a concept is and what it is not; examples and nonexamples may help him when interpreting questions.

• Using study guides as homework throughout the unit emphasizes the important facts and concepts of the unit and reinforces the material over time.

• Using peer tutoring and quick drills in class throughout the unit would also reinforce the important facts and concepts and help Josh's memory.

• By incorporating explicit learning strategies into their lessons, Josh's co-teachers could support his understanding of important facts and concepts and help other students at the same time.

I work with many individuals who have received unsatisfactory write-ups, quite possibly because their observers do not know how to properly assess the failures and successes of an inclusion classroom.

—*Elementary special education co-teacher*

I co-taught with a special education teacher during my second year of teaching. The principal observed both of us teach, but he did so separately. My co-teacher chose to have her observation during our co-taught class, while I chose to have my observation during a noninclusive class. The special education teacher taught our co-taught class by herself, while I sat in the back of the classroom, which is what the principal wanted to see.

—*High school general education co-teacher*

When I did my student teaching, I co-taught with a general education teacher and was concerned about how our supervisor would judge each of us. Eventually I was put at ease when a set of guidelines was created in order to make things clearer to all of us.

—*Middle school general education co-teacher*

As a first year administrator, I had no idea what to look for when observing a co-taught class. Luckily, my district had hired co-teacher consultants who walked me through an observation. I felt more secure after that—both in what I was doing to assist the co-teachers during the observation and at other times.

—*High school vice principal*

I am a special education supervisor who has had little experience with the earth science curriculum, but I do know how to recognize excellent co-teaching and am able to raise the level of the co-teaching experience in my school.

—*Middle school special education supervisor*

8

Defining and Assessing the Administrator's Role

Dr. Stevens, the principal of Central High, sighs as she enters the 11th grade social studies class. She generally likes the co-teaching program but finds it hard to evaluate individual teachers in co-teaching partnerships. The aim of the lesson is on the board, and the general education teacher, Ms. Nottingham, is explaining the Do Now as Ms. Halper, the special education teacher, distributes the handouts. For the lesson the students need to read a primary source of two speeches and then answer questions. After a few minutes, Ms. Nottingham discusses the readings and questions while Ms. Halper walks around the room. Ms. Nottingham lectures while Ms. Halper writes notes on the board. The lesson is interesting, well paced, and many students respond. Yet what is Ms. Halper's contribution to the class, Dr. Stevens wonders? Ms. Halper never took a lead role, the reading materials weren't adapted in any way for the students with reading difficulties, and none of the students with special needs participated in the discussions. Three of the seven students with special needs are failing the course. Dr. Stevens hates to, but she is going to give Ms. Halper an unsatisfactory rating for this lesson.

Ms. Halper, a nontenured second-year teacher, has worked for two years with Ms. Nottingham, an 18-year veteran teacher. Ms Halper worries that her evaluation will be negative because of Ms. Nottingham's reluctance to share the teaching responsibilities. Ms. Halper doesn't know how to discuss this problem with her. Ms. Nottingham is a fabulous teacher, but she rarely lets Ms. Halper do more than walk around and support the students. Ms. Halper does create some materials and offers to mark papers and call parents. Ms Nottingham usually says that the new materials will take too much time and water-down the content, and that she likes to mark the papers so she knows how all the students are doing. Ms. Nottingham only expects Ms. Halper to call the parents of the students with special needs. Ms. Halper feels a negative observation write-up would be unfair, and her future in this district is at stake because her co-teacher doesn't really embrace the program.

Why are administrators important in co-teaching?

At the forefront of inclusive settings are the general and special education administrators who must demonstrate leadership, enthusiasm, and determination to ensure effective teaching and adequate learning for all students. These are no small tasks. Administrators are in charge of scheduling the co-teaching classes, pairing co-teachers, and monitoring student progress. They must assign students with disabilities to the general education classes (being careful not to have a disproportionate number of classified students in a class); assign teachers to work together as co-teachers (being cognizant of the importance of a positive relationship); allocate scheduled planning time for the co-teachers (understanding that without co-planning there is limited effective co-teaching); and observe and evaluate the program (including the effectiveness of the teachers and the progress of students).

Administrators are called upon to set the tone and expectations of the school community and for the co-teaching program. Administrators are instrumental in merging students and teachers, both special education and general education. Clearly, the co-teaching model cannot be put into place and left alone. Administrative involvement and support are woven throughout the program, which requires ongoing commitment, a deep understanding about the learning needs of all students and strategies that support their learning, and the necessitation of adaptations and modifications to curriculum and assessment.

What do administrators have to do to set up an effective co-teaching program?

Inclusive programs that involve co-teaching demand a tremendous amount of administrative support. It's not an overstatement to say that without this support, a co-teaching program is bound to have more negatives than positives—and the potential losers are the students. Administrators must attend to many ongoing facets of the co-teaching program.

Selection of students for the inclusive co-taught class

Most of the successful programs that we've seen are the result of a reasonable proportion (between 20 and 30 percent) of students with disabilities in the co-taught class. As a precaution, avoid the propensity to put many students who are high risk for failure, but who are not yet classified as needing special education services, into a co-taught class. Although it's easy to identify the rationale for adding these students to the co-taught classroom—there are two teachers, and all students will be given individual and special attention—having too many students with needs (whether classified or not) in a class compromises the integrity and effectiveness of the program.

Scheduling students and teachers

Many successful programs use the co-taught classes to drive the rest of the master schedule. Assigning students and teachers to the co-taught classes first avoids the pitfalls of having to settle with second-best arrangements for students and teachers because of conflicting scheduling demands. We understand that this is a tall order, as some administrators are reluctant to place such priority on a single program. The differences between programs where co-taught inclusive classes are given priority versus those that don't receive priority are quite significant.

When co-teaching is not a priority, planning time for co-teachers is sacrificed; optimum pairing of co-teachers is jeopardized; unbalanced ratios between students with and without disabilities will occur; subject periods are not optimally scheduled; and room size is insufficient. When principals agree that co-teaching is a priority, content classes are often scheduled in the morning when students might be more alert (art and music may be scheduled in the afternoon); and larger classrooms that allow for easier parallel and station teaching are assigned to co-taught classes.

Selection of teacher pairs

Administrators and supervisors have two choices in forming teaching partnerships: asking teachers to volunteer or assigning teachers to co-teaching pairs. Sometimes teachers will volunteer for the position, but there must be a process for appropriate selection. Administrators must know the teachers and develop teachers' understanding and expertise in co-teaching. We've heard of instances in which teachers have not known that they are assigned to co-teach a class until the first day of school. Assignments made this way have little chance of success. If the administrator notifies the co-teachers in June and provides them with time during the summer to attend a workshop on co-teaching, then the co-teachers will have time to bond, plan, and discuss their goals for their co-taught class in the fall.

Underlying appropriate selection is the need for the administrators and supervisors to know each teacher's strengths and weaknesses. Voluntary participation is theoretically the best policy, as both teachers are committed to the co-teaching model. Necessity is sometimes the prevailing factor, however, and the administrator must determine if the selected teachers will act as equal partners. Some teachers are territorial and therefore not a great potential partner for tandem teaching. Administrators and supervisors must look for teachers who see how co-teaching benefits all students, are knowledgeable about content and process, are truly collaborative, and work toward the goal of success for every student.

Some first-year teachers are placed in co-teaching programs. Proponents of this practice state that it is beneficial for a new teacher to experience collaboration before becoming accustomed to a solo-taught class. Others believe that teachers should find their own way before being asked to collaborate with other teachers. We have witnessed first-year teachers who work together effectively as co-teachers, and we have noted the propensity for disparity in role sharing when a first-year teacher is paired with an experienced instructor. Administrators need to be cognizant of possible inequitable roles in any mix of co-teaching relationships and the likelihood of experienced teachers assuming a stronger role in the classroom than new teachers.

In reality, scheduling often plays a role in the assignment of co-teachers. Although understandable, and often unavoidable, this type of assignment can lead to inefficient and ineffective practices. Two teachers, virtually thrown together, can feel that they are on a year-long blind date. Negative feelings about the program may emerge and the support that is required for students to succeed is minimized.

Administrators also need to make the hard choice of ending a co-teaching relationship when the teachers are not getting along and the students are not achieving to expectations. The "divorce" needs to be done only after the administrator has observed and discussed the difficulties, tried counseling, listened to the co-teachers, and tried to resolve the problems (Murawski, 2010).

Schedule planning time

Without co-planning there is no co-teaching. Administrators must demonstrate the importance of the inclusion program and support co-teachers' efforts by providing time for the teachers to co-plan. Without allocated co-planning time, the general education teacher tends to do the planning, and the special education teacher is only marginally informed regarding the expectations and procedures of the class. When co-teachers plan together, there is a more positive ownership in the lesson and a shared ownership of the class. Each teacher is an equal in the success of all students' achievements. The administrator must support the co-teachers by showing how the planning time can be used most effectively.

Evaluate student progress

The bottom line of an inclusion program is how well the students are succeeding in their individual pursuits of learning. A vigilant administrator tracks student performance on state-mandated assessments and report card grades, and monitors IEP performance goals.

Observe and supervise co-teachers

Administrators and supervisors must provide supportive observation and supervision by understanding the dynamics of co-teaching, recognizing the adaptations made prior to the lesson, and encouraging effective co-teaching practices. The administrator or supervisor needs to remember to observe the co-teachers as a unit, not as individual teachers.

Promote professional development

Administrative support of co-teachers involves providing access to seminars, programs, consultants, videos, and books that describe and portray effective co-teaching.

Propagate understanding of inclusive programs among other administrators and supervisors

Administrators knowledgeable about co-teaching make every effort to dispel myths and educate others on the positive aspects of co-teaching inclusive programs. They can do this using multiple avenues. For example, one principal met with all chairs and supervisors responsible for observing co-teachers during the summer. He gave them the guidelines in Figure 8.1 to be used when observing the tandem teachers. The co-teachers were also given these guidelines. Everyone knew what was expected of him or her. During the year, the principal sent chairpersons, supervisors, and co-teachers to workshops and arranged for them to visit schools that had successful co-teaching programs. Once a month, this principal also met with everyone involved in co-teaching to discuss successes and concerns.

Develop parent understanding of inclusive programs

Through meetings of parent-teacher associations of both general education students and special education students (PTA and SEPTA) and individual interactions with parents, administrators actively support an understanding of the inclusion program.

Problem solve co-teaching and inclusion issues as they arise

Teachers are often left to settle difficult issues themselves. Administrators should be part of the ongoing growth of co-teachers and help develop understanding and effective practices. Reviewing hypothetical vignettes can lead to innovative ways of solving problems and is a means of keeping communication channels open.

In one school, the building administrators developed a school climate conducive to the co-teaching staff. Although this school's co-teaching program began with only four pairs of co-teachers on one grade level, they were given workshops on how to successfully co-teach. As part of the reward for being progressive and trying out co-teaching, those teachers were the first recipients of interactive white boards and were granted staff development hours to learn how to use them. The administrators videotaped the co-taught teachers while they were using the new technology and the best video examples of co-teaching were shared with the entire faculty. Co-teachers became instant faculty stars and they were proud of their accomplishment. The school reports that several additional teachers volunteered to co-teach the next year.

Figure 8.1 | Co-Teaching Observation Guide

The following questions may serve as self-reflective questions for the co-teachers and also focus an observer or supervisor on the unique aspects of co-teaching.

I. The Basics: Meaningful Roles for Each Teacher

1. Can the role of each teacher be defined at any given point in the lesson?
2. Is each role meaningful? Does each role enhance the learning process?
3. Do the teachers vary their roles during the course of the lesson?
4. Is each teacher well suited to the role(s) he or she is assuming?
5. Are both teachers comfortable with process and content?
6. Is the special education teacher working with all students?

II. Strategies to Promote Success for All Students

1. What evidence is there that teachers engaged in co-planning the lesson?
2. Are the teachers focusing on process as well as content?
3. Are they reinforcing important skills?
4. Are directions clear?
5. What strategies or modifications are used to assist struggling students?
6. What adaptations were made to materials to help struggling students complete tasks?
7. What strategies are being used to actively engage students?
8. How are students being grouped? Does it fit the task? Is it purposeful?
9. What reinforcement strategies are being employed?

III. Evidence of Success

1. Are struggling students answering and asking questions?
2. Are students engaged in meaningful work throughout the period?
3. How are teachers assessing the learning of each student?
4. What evidence is there that all students have been appropriately challenged?

Source: Wilson, G. L. (2005). This doesn't look familiar! A supervisor's guide for observing co-teachers. *Intervention in School and Clinic, 40*(5), 271–275. p. 272. Reprinted with permission. © 2005 SAGE Publications, Inc.

What if parents strongly oppose or insist on the placement of their child in the co-taught setting?

If a parent opposes the co-taught placement for a typically achieving child, the administrator needs to listen to the parent and analyze the concerns. Change is what scares parents. If the administrator takes the time to talk with parents and to identify the positive aspects of a co-taught class, she can alleviate many misgivings. If the parent is not convinced that the co-taught class is the best placement for the student, the administrator may want to have the parent meet the co-teachers to discuss any concerns that linger. The co-teachers can identify the positive aspects of being in a co-taught class—including the availability of two adult teachers in the classroom to assist all students at all times, and their ability to implement multiple learning strategies while providing multiple pathways to learning. In addition, a co-teaching classroom helps to prepare students for a diverse world and to increase tolerance.

Parents of a typically achieving student are not required by any federal law or regulation to accept their child's placement in a co-taught classroom. Few district policies require that the parents of typically achieving students accept their child's placement in a co-taught classroom. If parents of a typically achieving child want him or her switched from a co-taught to a traditional class, it generally rests with the principal to weigh in and decide to go along with the parent or hold firm. Principals can easily identify the many positives of a co-taught class and often elicit a positive response from the parents.

If the parents of a student with special needs do not want their child placed in a co-taught class and prefer or demand a different special education program, they have to work through the Committee on Special Education process and either agree with the placement on their child's IEP or use their due process rights to contest the placement. If parents of a student with an IEP disagree with the placement, federal safeguards under IDEIA provide due process procedures for students and parents. Parents of special needs students do have options when disagreements arise regarding student placement. In a case where the parents want their child in a co-taught class, and the school wants the child in a self-contained class, the parent or district may return to the CSE for further discussion and negotiation on options, which might include a trial placement in the co-taught class.

Requests from parents are many and varied:

• A parent of a 6th grade student with special needs wanted her child placed in a co-taught classroom, but she requested that her child and another student with special needs not be assigned to the same classroom. The two students had been together since 1st grade and had a history of being hostile toward each other. Both students were originally scheduled for the only 6th grade co-taught class. After discussions with both sets of parents, the co-teachers, and the administration, this situation was resolved by placing both students in the co-taught class with the stipulation that the co-teachers would separate the students as often as possible.

• A parent of a 12th grade typically achieving student wanted his child placed in a general education English class: "My child is too intelligent to be in a co-taught class. I want his last year at high school to be his best!" All English 12 classes at this school were co-taught. This situation was resolved by educating the parent about the many advantages of a co-taught class. The parent rescinded her objections, and the student attended the co-taught English class.

How can administrators help teachers to understand the complexities of administering a co-taught program?

Despite the best intentions, student ratios may not be the most favorable, co-teaching pairs are not optimal, planning time is not sufficient, or some other aspect of the program may not be most advantageous. Open communication with teachers, parents, and students may promote an understanding of the complexities confronting the administration of an inclusive program. If stakeholders know that the difficulties are at least understood by administration and that efforts to address the problems are made in good faith, negative feelings can be mitigated. Administrators must assess the success of the co-taught class several times during the school year. When problems develop, the administrator must step in to solve the problems. When co-teachers understand that the administration is supportive and willing to work through problems, co-teachers feel comfortable about voicing their opinions and finding solutions together. For instance, co-teachers found the size of their co-taught classroom inadequate for 26 desks. When the co-teachers communicated their concern, the administrator was able to replace the desks with science tables and stools that were found in storage.

How do administrators and supervisors observe co-teachers?

Many co-teachers and supervisors are confused about what exactly is expected within the co-taught setting. Often, the blatant differences between what general and special education supervisors look for in a co-taught class send mixed messages to the co-teachers. In addition, co-teachers often have different perceptions about their roles and effectiveness, as well as their willingness to embrace new skills such as adapting lesson plans, shifting classroom management, adjusting professional interactions, and adapting instruction.

Evaluation and supervision processes are usually mandated by the teachers' contracts and need to be followed. Some surprises may be lurking in what may be considered standard yet outdated language. For example, some districts prohibit an observing supervisor from mentioning another teacher in the report, underscoring the need for administrators and supervisors to understand that co-teaching is not two teachers separately engaged in a classroom. Co-teaching is what happens when two teachers are essentially linked with each other, and observations should always reflect the interactions and importance of both teachers.

Administrators are faced with adjusting supervisory and evaluation techniques when shifting from traditional solo-taught to innovative co-taught settings. A reflective guide for supervision is shown in Figure 8.1, the Co-Teaching Observation Guide. The guide (Wilson, 2005) provides a series of questions for the administrator and the co-teaching pair to consider when co-teaching. The guide was developed by supervisors and teachers as a way of focusing attention on the roles, strategies, and assessment of co-teaching, and it provides a structure for co-teachers to use when planning and reflecting on their practice. Administrators and supervisors can use the guide to focus on the important elements of co-teaching. Collaborative supervision (described next) is another important way to attend to the supervision and observation of co-teaching.

If two different supervisors are responsible for the co-teachers, we recommend that they observe the co-teachers and write a report together. Tandem practice highlights the importance of the collaborative efforts by the co-teachers and also strengthens a unified message from the supervisors.

How is collaborative supervision done?

To provide for a common foundation for observing co-taught classes, we suggest collaborative supervision and evaluation. Goldhammer (1983) envisioned the supervisory challenge to include teachers in the process to ensure a more meaningful and effective learning situation in a nonthreatening environment. Collaborative supervision, though not devised for co-teaching, is an effective model for co-teaching supervision and evaluation because the focus is on the co-teachers and the administrators working together to advance learning in the classroom. The process directs the administration and co-teachers to schedule time together to mutually discuss goals, challenges, and roles, and to observe and reflect upon classroom practices in an effort to raise the level of learning for all students.

Traditional supervision is usually relegated to a specified number of lesson observations and reports spaced throughout the school year with a formal pre-observation, observation, and post-observation sequence done multiple times throughout the year. By creating a collegial atmosphere in which the administrators and co-teachers are partners in the process, everyone can participate in meaningful ongoing discussions and reflections that allow for problem solving, adjustment, and follow-up throughout the year.

Collaborative supervision is a flexible process. First, the administrators and co-teachers meet to review goals, concerns, and plans for the upcoming classroom observation. Together, in a nonjudgmental and collegial setting, goals are discussed in terms of their achievability and practicality. The co-teaching classroom is a conducive location for a relaxed discussion and gives the administrators a peek into the working environment of the co-teachers. As a bonus, influences from both teachers are present in the classroom. At the meeting, general goals and concerns are discussed, and then the co-teachers present their plan for the upcoming observation. Besides addressing the components of what typically makes up a "good" lesson, such as motivation, content, and management, the co-teachers need to focus on their defined roles, instructional strategies, and assessment processes.

After the lesson, the administrators and the co-teachers are asked to consider the delivery of the lesson and the performance of the co-teachers. Are they equal, respectful partners? Do they meet the needs of each student in the class? What is their ability to assess student learning and growth? The classroom observation is followed by a post-observation conference with discussion and reflection on each teacher's strengths and areas that need to be addressed. Collaborative supervision and evaluation becomes a trust-building exercise that provides a rewarding, solid foundation for teacher and administrator growth that ultimately results in increased student learning.

One supervisory team using collaborative supervision videotaped a series of the co-teachers in the classroom. The video was a terrific way for the teachers to observe themselves and their interactions with each other and with their students. The team felt the video was invaluable both as a validation of what they already suspected was a positive inclusive classroom and as a means to improve their practice.

How can districts gather evidence on the effectiveness of co-teaching?

Determining if co-teaching efforts are leading to successful student learning and progress can be problematic. Information garnered by gathering IQ scores, achievement test scores, testing modifications, related services, report card grades, and performances on high-stakes tests of classified students in co-taught classes can lead to an analysis of the effectiveness of co-teaching. While broad measures such as report card grades don't show the nuances of learning that are taking place, they do reveal whether students are successfully meeting the demands of general education settings, which is the ultimate goal of co-teaching.

Districts will find supporting evidence for co-teaching programs as they supply appropriate professional development, set up curriculum-based and other measures of student progress, review discipline referrals, and track the long-term performance of students (Friend & Hurley-Chamberlain, n.d.).

How do large-scale, high-stakes testing affect co-teaching?

Requiring students to take large-scale state or national tests intended to assess student, teacher, or school performance is controversial. Everyone agrees that expectations for all students should be high, but the adequacy or fairness of mandated tests is often questioned. Some teachers point to the pressures of these tests on students and teachers alike and how preparing for the assessments takes time away from authentic learning. The assessments are often used to identify students who need additional instructional supports, rate teachers on their effectiveness, and compare schools and school districts.

Historically, waivers were given to classified students with the rationale that because of specific disabilities, the standards did not hold. It became apparent that expectations for students with disabilities were lower, as the performance achievement gap became wider. *Those who are not tested are not counted* became an overriding cry from members of the special education community as they lobbied to include students with disabilities in large-scale, high-stakes testing. No longer did special educators want the deficiencies or low expectations of the system to be ignored or go unnoticed. The No Child Left Behind Act and the Individuals with Disabilities Improvement Act now require the participation of students with disabilities in state and district assessments.

Questions remain about the fairness of the assessments for students with disabilities. Among the concerns are the possibility of students with disabilities performing poorly on the assessments and being at risk for increased grade retention or dropping out of school. Bowen and Rude (2006) contend that, although the task is difficult, there can be an alignment of goals, expectations, and assessments between NCLB with IDEIA 2004, both of which attempt to shrink the achievement gap of students with disabilities. Despite concerns, there are some signs of progress with participation of students with disabilities steadily increasing (Thompson & Thurlow, 2001) and some correlation between improved access and performance (Ysseldyke et al., 2004). In New York State, for instance, more students with special needs are passing the Regents exams (high school content exams) than had ever traditionally taken them before NCLB and IDEIA (Gloeckler, 2001). Students in co-taught classes are at an advantage because of the increased opportunities to learn and the increased intensity of support afforded to them in the inclusive setting.

What happens if students with special needs in co-taught classes don't do well on high-stakes testing?

The complexities and controversial issues surrounding large-scale, high-stakes testing for students with disabilities are many, including ensuring that students are given access to high-quality instruction and the general education curriculum, students are afforded appropriate accommodations, and measures of adequate yearly progress are accurate (Bowen & Rude, 2006). In many respects, high-stakes tests assess the very deficiencies manifested by students with disabilities. A student reading at the 8th percentile will surely not do well on an English Language Arts state exam without accommodations, no matter what the expectations. This student, even with intensive and high-quality instruction provided by co-teachers, might make minimal progress within a given year and perform poorly on the ELA exam. That sort of result can be particularly problematic for co-teachers who are increasingly being held accountable for the progress of all students.

Doing poorly on a high-stakes test does not necessarily indicate poor teaching or poor student effort. Unfortunately, these possibilities are only marginally addressed and the potential consequence is that some teachers may be unwilling to teach in inclusive classes for fear of negative ramifications when students with special needs do not adequately perform. Much more thoughtful discourse concerning the need for high expectations, excellent teaching, and an understanding of the individual complexities of learning difficulties needs to inform policies regarding testing as they pertain to students with disabilities.

Case Study 15

How can supervisors give consistent messages and evaluations to increase effectiveness of a co-taught inclusion program?

Ms. Hessnah, the special education co-teacher, wants to incorporate different strategies into her 7th grade social studies class. Her co-teacher, Mr. Simon, insists that students in the class must be able to learn the curriculum the way that he usually teaches it. The department chair says that Mr. Simon should not have to change his teaching in any way and that if the students do not succeed, then it is apparent that they don't belong in an inclusive setting. In addition to these conflicts, the co-teachers do not share the same philosophy on grading. Mr. Simon believes that grades are earned, as does the chair. Ms. Hessnah feels obligated to adapt and modify tests in compliance with the IEPs of the students in the class.

In one instance, the social studies chair and special education chair observed the class at the same time. The write-ups were completely different. The special education chair commented on the lack of adaptive strategies and the passive role of the special education teacher. The social studies chair commented on the good pacing of the class and Mr. Simon's command of the curriculum and the class.

Statement of the problem

Ms. Hessnah and Mr. Simon have different ideas about their roles and the needs of their students.

Problem genesis

The supervisors are working at cross purposes and are reinforcing conflicting attitudes.

How the problem is being denied or addressed

Ms. Hessnah's ability to teach is being compromised by a negative observation report and Mr. Simon's beliefs. Ultimately, the students suffer.

Ways to promote a positive outcome

• The supervisors are off to a good start by co-observing the same lesson. The practice of co-observing can lead to increased communication and understanding for co-teachers and supervisors.

• Although both supervisors observed the lesson, they missed the opportunity to discuss their observations and concerns. If they talked to the co-teachers before and after the observation regarding what they were looking for and their expectations, they would have uncovered some of the conflicting goals and expectations that they have for their teachers.

• The supervisors have a responsibility to reach common ground on co-teaching fundamentals, including expectations for students, understanding the differences between inclusion and mainstreaming, the importance of following IEP dictates, the belief that special education is a service and not a place, and the belief that special education strategies are needed in the inclusive classroom.

• Most teachers work hard to satisfy the demands from supervisors. Clear and specific goals that are common to both the general education and special education supervisors must be in place to avoid mixed messages and resulting teacher conflicts.

————————•●•————————

Case Study 16

How can administrative issues of parity be resolved?

Ms. Tashini and Ms. Rush co-teach 6th grade language arts classes. They co-plan their lessons, share in the grading responsibilities, and take turns calling parents. On the students' schedules and report cards, only Ms. Tashini's name appears. When Ms. Rush, the special education teacher, is absent, no substitute is hired. A substitute is always supplied in Ms. Tashini's absence. Ms. Rush is sometimes asked to leave the co-taught language arts class for an emergency assignment.

Statement of the problem

The special education co-teacher feels that her presence in the co-taught inclusion class is expendable.

Problem genesis

Administrative actions using the special education co-teacher to cover classes, failing to get a substitute for her, and not having her name on the schedule or report cards provides a foundation for unequal status between the teachers and in the eyes of others.

How the problem is being denied or addressed

The policies are being tolerated, but damage to the co-teaching inclusion program will persist if changes aren't made.

Ways of promoting a positive outcome

• A campaign by the co-teachers (preferably all co-teachers in the building) to inform the administration of the inequities is imperative. The practices might not be intentional and might be readily fixed.

• If an integrated co-teaching program is stipulated on the IEP, then two teachers need to be in the classroom. Not hiring a substitute for the special education teacher or asking her to cover other classes is not legally compliant.

I find my position as a paraprofessional to be both interesting and rewarding. I always take my directions from the co-teachers and do exactly what I am directed to do. I would never want to be the teacher. That job is too hard and demands too much personal time.

—*Middle school paraprofessional*

I am an underpaid and underappreciated paraprofessional. I do all the jobs that the teachers don't want to do, like reading tests to students. Teachers get all the money and I do all the work.

—*High school paraprofessional*

I don't know what we would do without the paraeducator in our room. She goes well beyond what is expected and is incredible in every way. The students love her and because of her efforts, they are much more successful.

—*Elementary co-teacher*

In my experience as a co-teacher, there are only two paraprofessionals in my building whom I welcome into my classroom. These two enhance the learning of my students, while the other paraprofessionals act as distractions to students. Why aren't co-teachers asked to reveal which paraprofessional they think work best within their classroom?

—*High school co-teacher*

My district always does it wrong. The co-teaching model used here is one general education teacher with one special education teacher every other day; a paraprofessional is in the room on alternate days. Can you believe this district thinks a paraprofessional can replace a certified special education teacher?

—*Middle school general education teacher*

9

Clarifying the Paraprofessional's Role

Ms. Sanchez, a paraprofessional hired to shadow a 3rd grade student with autism spectrum disorder (ASD), waits for him to arrive at school. At first, she was apprehensive having to be with a student all day, particularly a student with ASD. She wasn't given any training, just directions to be with Josh for the entire day. A few weeks later, Ms. Sanchez is confident in her ability to work with Josh. He is prone to verbal outbreaks particularly when routines change, but Ms. Sanchez responds by taking him out of the classroom to calm him down. In the morning, Josh's mom tells Ms. Sanchez if he is having a rough morning or alerts her to something that might be going on at home that might distress him. In the afternoon, Ms. Sanchez briefly recounts the events of the day to Josh's mom.

The co-teachers notice that Ms. Sanchez talks with Josh's mother in the parking lot. At first they were happy that Ms. Sanchez was taking the time to communicate with Josh's mother, but now they are wondering if Ms. Sanchez is going beyond her role as a paraprofessional. Both are concerned about what Ms. Sanchez says to Josh's mom. Lately Josh's mom sends notes to school addressed to Ms. Sanchez, and the co-teachers have to ask to see the notes. Ms. Elington and Ms. Paquale are beginning to realize that they have pretty much left Josh's education to Ms. Sanchez. Ms. Sanchez explains and adapts materials, oversees his work, takes Josh away from the group when he is not focused, sits next to him in class, and packs his knapsack for him at the end of the day. The co-teachers are thinking that maybe it's time to reassess their roles in Josh's school experience.

Who is a paraprofessional?

A paraprofessional is a district employee who is not required to be licensed to teach, but performs many duties both individually with students and organizationally within the school and classroom. A paraprofessional's work supports teachers and assists students, but this employee is not directly responsible for planning or teaching. The Committee on Special Education often assigns a paraprofessional to a student with special needs whose particular behaviors, learning needs, or physical needs warrant close supervision and assistance.

Paraprofessionals vary in training from limited education courses to graduate degrees in education, and district policies on hiring paraprofessionals vary with the mandates of the state. Under ideal circumstances, having a certified, enthusiastic, well-prepared paraprofessional can make an enormous difference in the efficiency of the classroom and the implementation of a student's IEP.

What qualifications are needed to be a paraprofessional?

Federal regulations require new paraprofessionals to have two years of higher education, or an associate's degree, or demonstrate an ability to assist students in basic academic skills (U.S. Department of Education, 2005). However, each school district hires paraprofessionals depending on state regulations and adheres to the requirements of the local state education department. If the paraprofessionals in the district are unionized, conditions for the contract must also be satisfied. With a surplus of teachers looking for employment in a geographic area, the district may hire a certified teacher as a paraprofessional.

Requirements for paraprofessionals vary from state to state. For example, to earn a New York State certificate as a teaching assistant/paraprofessional, candidates must complete an application, pay a fee, and pass the Assessment of Teaching Assistant Skills exam. The exam is a four-hour multiple-choice, criterion-referenced, and objective-based exam divided into reading, writing, mathematics, and instructional support. In addition, there are three levels of paraprofessional certification (New York State Education Department, 2006).

States and districts have disparate demands for the training and certification of paraprofessionals. For example, in Minnesota, paraprofessionals are required to have two years or 60 credits from an institute of higher learning, or an associate's degree, or pass a formal state or local assessment. In Louisiana, paraprofessionals need a high school diploma and must pass a paraprofessional test or earn 48 hours of credits from an institute of higher learning, a technical diploma for paraprofessionals, or an associate's or baccalaureate degree. California has raised its standards so that being a paraprofessional is an official stepping stone to becoming a certified teacher. Clearly, anyone hiring or working with a paraprofessional should be aware of the specific requirements in the district and state. And it's important for everyone to be aware of the training and experience these professionals offer in any classroom situation, particularly in a co-teaching classroom.

What type of guidance increases paraprofessional effectiveness in the co-taught classroom?

Paraprofessionals rarely receive formal professional development in co-teaching, which undermines the important role that they can play in the school community. Although extensive training is not necessary, paraprofessionals and co-teachers benefit from a session at the beginning of the year that outlines roles and responsibilities and gives general information on the variety of learning and behavior difficulties of the students in the co-taught classroom. Classroom-specific training may be done by an administrator, supervisor, consultant, or the co-teachers themselves. Additional professional development sessions with teachers and paraprofessionals throughout the school year give the paraprofessionals some voice and a chance to learn helpful strategies. In addition, co-teachers should meet with the paraprofessionals early in the year to go over IEPs. Although confidentiality must always be maintained, inviting the paraprofessional to participate in meetings with parents and guidance counselors is appropriate and useful.

At the very least, paraprofessionals should be given precise directions every day by the co-teachers. For example, in a co-taught 4th grade class, two paraprofessionals are also part of the classroom. The co-teachers devised a plan by which one co-teacher gave clear and concise directions regarding the day's lessons to the paraprofessionals while the other co-teacher took attendance, checked homework, and started the students on the day's morning work. Communicating the day's expectations ensured that all adults in the classroom were working together to achieve common goals, and the paraprofessionals were able to be effective and comfortable in their roles.

What are the roles of paraprofessionals?

Paraprofessionals are usually hired by the school district's special education supervisor to assist students who need support as mandated by their IEP. A paraprofessional can support students with disabilities by monitoring behavior, providing individual and small-group instruction to reinforce what was taught by the co-teachers, and sometimes providing an important connection between parents and the classroom. Paraprofessionals may be hired for a wide range of roles.

Paraprofessionals may shadow a student with disabilities. A student may need the assistance of a paraprofessional to get from class to class safely and on time. Once in class, the paraprofessional helps the student get seated, lays out the materials for the lesson, and prepares to help the student engage in instruction. The paraprofessional may also shadow the student in large-group settings, including the cafeteria, physical education classes, and assemblies and fire drills. Paraprofessionals are also valuable in helping their students embark and disembark the school bus.

Paraprofessionals may organize students. Paraprofessionals remind students to write homework assignments in their assignment book, take the proper books home for assignments, and study for upcoming exams.

Paraprofessionals may alternate with the special education co-teacher. Given budget cuts, some districts have become creative in their scheduling. Some districts schedule special education teachers as a co-teacher on the first of a two-day cycle, with a paraprofessional providing instructional support on day two. Other districts have the special education co-teacher in the class for half a day, with the paraprofessional in the class for the other half of the day. Most co-teachers feel these arrangements are problematic and have a negative effect on student learning.

Paraprofessionals may connect with parents and community. Since many paraprofessionals live in the school district in which they work, they often interact with parents at the local supermarket, house of worship, movie theater, or restaurant (Chopra & French, 2004). The paraprofessional's role outside the school may be expanded if his or her cultural knowledge and language proficiencies match those of the community and parents, especially if the co-teachers' backgrounds and languages are not a match.

What is expected of paraprofessionals?

Administrators, co-teachers, parents, and students all have unique expectations for paraprofessionals.

• Administrators expect that the students' instructional needs, as well as their safety and well-being, are supported by paraprofessionals.

• Co-teachers rely on paraprofessionals to discreetly keep students focused, organized, and on task.

• Parents expect paraprofessionals to attend to students' needs and to provide individual support in inclusive settings, as per the IEP.

• Students with special needs often expect assistance organizing their notes, handouts, desks, backpacks, homework, and study materials. Students also frequently rely on the paraprofessional to answer specific questions concerning the lesson.

Paraprofessionals themselves have expectations of their roles and know that they are a valuable resource and want to be respected team members. If given too much responsibility, they may feel they are assuming the role of the teacher without commensurate pay. On the flip side, if paraprofessionals are given too little responsibility or guidance, they can feel underused and undervalued.

To capitalize on the contributions from paraprofessionals, clear roles and guidance need to be established by the school district, the school, and the co-teachers. Roles and expectations for the paraprofessionals, including strict confidentiality sanctions, need to be clear and workable in the classroom. Professional development training for all those involved, including teachers, paraprofessionals, and administrators, is imperative for the paraprofessional co-teaching model to succeed. For example, in one elementary school, paraprofessionals are considered part of the faculty. Paraprofessionals attend faculty meetings and other meetings with parents and guidance counselors, and they receive professional development training with the co-teachers throughout the year. They are respected for the work that they do with students. In this supportive environment, the paraprofessionals work hard to help the students succeed.

In another elementary school in the same district, the paraprofessionals are given little direction and are not included in any professional activity. The paraprofessionals in this school feel invisible and unappreciated; as a result, their important work is diminished. Shared professional development and understanding of expectations on all levels may improve this situation, as well as expanding the learning opportunities for the students.

What types of relationships do paraprofessionals have with parents?

At least four types of relationships form between paraprofessionals and the parents of students with disabilities (French & Chopra, 1999). As a connector, paraprofessionals communicate with parents about their child, sometimes as often as daily. As a team member, paraprofessionals work with their student more closely than anyone else in the school and are valuable participants in planning (with the teachers) and also communicating that information to parents. As an instructor, the paraprofessional reinforces the instruction provided by the co-teachers and needs to explain this role to the parents. And, in the physical aspects of the job, paraprofessionals need to relate to parents as a physical caretaker of their child at school.

What cautions and advice are most helpful for working with and being a paraprofessional in a co-taught class?

A co-taught classroom can be a crowded place. Imagine two teachers, a paraprofessional or two, and an observing supervisor. All parties must be aware of all the roles being played in the classroom and carry out their own roles effectively. With planning and precision, multiple adults can work together to benefit all students. The co-teachers must take a leadership role in designating different tasks to each of the other adults in the classroom. In a well-orchestrated classroom, everyone knows that all their efforts will contribute to the achievement of the students.

Unfortunately, many co-teachers do not understand their role in directing paraprofessionals. Of course, it can be difficult for co-teachers to assume a supervisory role if they haven't had any planning time or supervisory training. Intuitively, it may seem that the more hands helping in a co-taught class, the better the learning, but this is not necessarily the case. Reflecting on the helping or hindering aspects of multiple adults in the classroom, Giangreco, Edelman, Luiselli and MacFarland (1997) highlight the negative effects of "hovering" and suggest school districts rethink their policies, practices, and training. See Figure 9.1 for categories of behaviors and responses a paraprofessional must be careful to avoid in the classroom. Specifically, paraprofessionals must not take on roles or responsibilities of the co-teachers, inadvertently segregate or limit the interactions of a student with special needs from classmates, limit competent instruction, or interfere with the instruction of other students (Giangreco, 2010).

What should be done if a paraprofessional goes beyond the boundaries of the role?

Paraprofessionals in the school district, school, and co-taught classroom need to have clear guidelines that protect the paraprofessional and address student safety. The guidelines go far beyond background checks, testing, and fingerprint clearance.

Mary, a paraprofessional, working one-on-one with Donna, an 8th grade middle school student, enjoyed her private talks with Donna. Mary liked feeling important, being a "cool" adult and learning about Donna's life. Donna was a troubled girl who found Mary to be the only adult with whom she could talk. Donna confided that she was using drugs. Mary did her best to talk Donna out of using drugs and promised not tell the co-teachers, the guidance counselor, or Donna's parent. One weekend Donna overdosed on drugs and needed to be hospitalized. Mary clearly did not understand her responsibility to alert authorities. There is no confidentiality between a student and a paraprofessional or between a student and any school employee when the health and welfare of a minor is at stake. The school principal immediately fired Mary for endangering the safety and well-being of a minor. Donna's story emphasizes the need for clear and specific guidelines for the paraprofessional. In this case, the school must assume part of the blame for not clarifying boundaries for the paraprofessionals. Everyone hired to care for children must understand that the safety and well being of those children is their primary responsibility.

Figure 9.1 | Inadvertent Detrimental Effects of Excessive Paraprofessional Proximity

Category of effect	Description
Separation from classmates	Student with a disability and paraprofessional are seated in the back or side of the room, physically separated from the class.
Unnecessary dependence	Student with a disability is hesitant to participate without paraprofessional direction, prompting, or cueing.
Interference with peer interaction	Paraprofessionals can create physical or symbolic barriers interfering with interactions between a student with disabilities and classmates.
Insular relationships	Student with a disability and paraprofessional do most everything together, to the exclusion of others (e.g., peers).
Feelings of stigmatization	Student with a disability expresses embarrassment/discomfort about having a paraprofessional because it makes him/her standout in negative ways.
Limited access to competent instruction	Paraprofessionals are not always skilled in providing instruction. Some do the work for the students they support in an effort to keep up (a sign that instruction has not been adequately adapted).
Interference with teacher engagement	Teachers tend to be less involved when a student with a disability has a one-to-one paraprofessional because individual attention is already available to the student.
Loss of personal control	Paraprofessionals do so much for the students with disabilities that they do not exercise choices that are typical of other students.
Loss of gender identity	Student with a disability is treated as the gender of the paraprofessional (e.g., male taken into female bathroom).
Provocation of problem behaviors	Some students with disabilities express their dislike of paraprofessional support by displaying undesirable behaviors (e.g., running away, foul language, aggression).
Risk of being bullied	Some students are teased or bullied because they are assigned a paraprofessional.

Source: Giangreco, M. F. (2010). One-to-one paraprofessionals for students with disabilities in inclusive classrooms: Is conventional wisdom wrong? *Intellectual and Developmental Disabilities, 48*(1), 1–12. p. 5. Reprinted with permission. © 2010 American Association on Intellectual Developmental Disabilities. All rights reserved.

Case Study 17

How can we ensure appropriate roles for paraprofessionals in the co-taught class?

Ms. Akaia is a one-to-one aide for Jonathan, a student with ASD. Ms. Akaia sits right next to Jonathan and assists him as he attempts to do the class assignments. She makes sure he has a pen and is following along with the class directions and lecture. She redirects his attention and keeps him on task. Neither co-teacher comes around to interact with Jonathan. The co-teachers expect Ms. Akaia to make sure that Jonathan is learning.

Statement of the problem

Co-teachers are abdicating their responsibilities to teach all students on their class roster by holding expectations of the paraprofessional beyond her job description.

Problem genesis

The co-teachers may feel that with a one-on-one paraprofessional, the class has one less student that they have to worry about. Administration has not provided clear delineation of responsibilities and accountability.

How the problem is being denied or addressed

The co-teachers are comfortable having the paraprofessional take on significant teaching responsibilities.

Ways of promoting a positive outcome

• Administrators must have written descriptions of the role a paraprofessional plays in the co-taught class, and the responsibilities of the co-teachers need to be understood and accepted by all the adults in the classroom.

• Co-teachers need to explain to the student that the paraprofessional is there to assist him or her; however, the co-teachers are there for all the students and will also work with each and every student in the class.

Case Study 18

How can we increase the effectiveness of a paraprofessional in the classroom?

Mr. Mikaella is a paraprofessional in a co-taught class. A certified teacher who is hoping to get a full-time teaching job in the district, Mr. Mikaella is assigned to various co-taught classes on a rotating basis and is in each of the classes on alternate days. He never knows what is going to be taught on any given day. He rarely gets a greeting from either of the co-teachers and tends to sit in the back of the class waiting for some direction.

Statement of problem

As a paraprofessional, Mr. Mikaella does not know what he is supposed to be doing in the classrooms.

Problem genesis

No one has given clear guidelines about the role of a paraprofessional in the classroom.

How the problem is being denied or addressed

Placing paraprofessionals in multiple classrooms and requiring them to adjust to various conditions without planning indicates that all parties (administrators, teachers, and paraprofessionals) are denying that there is a problem.

Ways to promote a positive outcome

• Clear lines of communication need to be set up between the co-teachers and the paraprofessional.

• The administration should set clear duties and expectations for paraprofessionals and needs to communicate them to everyone.

• The administration needs to limit the number of different assignments given to each paraprofessional. For example, a paraprofessional may be given the assignment to work in only 11th grade U.S. history. Narrowing the focus to one subject enables the paraprofessional to know or learn the curriculum being taught.

• A weekly planning session, even if held after school hours, enables Mr. Mikaella to know what is being taught in the classrooms and help make his role meaningful.

• The paraprofessional needs to feel like he is contributing to the success of the class by understanding and knowing what is being taught, as well as which students need his assistance and how he can assist them.

My child never liked being in the self-contained special education class. He felt it was for dummies and he felt segregated from the *real* student body. I jumped at the chance to have him placed in a co-taught class. The results were amazing. My son is happy to go to school and he is doing better than I ever dreamed possible.

—*Parent of a middle school student*

I don't know why everyone doesn't want his or her child in a co-taught class. My child did so well and was able to learn more than he would have in a general education class. He received individual learning for an entire year. It was a true gift.

—*Parent of a middle school student*

My friend from SEPTA encouraged me to place my son in a co-taught class. What a difference in the education of my child. His co-teachers were caring and fun and my son successfully passed his first Regents exam. He now feels he is smart and can do the work of high school. Thank you.

—*Parent of a high school student*

For the first time I'm in a general ed class and I love it!

—*High school student with special needs in a co-taught class*

I like both of my teachers and am getting a *B* in math.

—*Middle school student with special needs in a co-taught class*

I like all the strategies my teachers use to help us learn the information. We go into groups and I participate a lot.

—*High school student in a co-taught class*

10

Addressing Parent and Student Issues

Ms. Diaz is the mother of 14-year-old Nathan, a high school freshman. She reminisces about Nathan's success at the 52-student private school for children with severe dyslexia. He had worked hard and progress was slow, but Nathan now has skills that he and his parents once thought were unattainable. As she walks into the high school (with 2,000 students) to enroll her son in 9th grade, she cannot help but be concerned. How is Nathan ever going to survive four years? He is so used to one-on-one instruction that she worries whether co-taught classes will offer enough support. She's been assured that Nathan would be in good hands, but Ms. Diaz knows that school will always be a challenge for him and how crucial it is for him to be supported in co-taught classes. Ms. Diaz takes a deep breath as she signs the enrollment forms.

Nathan, an intelligent, social, handsome, athletic 14-year-old, worries about fitting in with the track team at his new school. He is proud of finishing first for his age bracket in the last triathlon and hopes that his classmates will focus on his running skills and not his reading skills. It's taken Nathan a long time to acquire basic reading skills, and the private school for students with dyslexia helped. But now he'll be in a school of 2,000 students. Nathan had only nine friends in his old school and thinks how many more friends he can have now. He is nervous and afraid and wants to get through the year without getting bad grades. Nathan works hard and knows that he will have to ask teachers for help when he doesn't understand things. He loved his old school but can hardly believe he will be going to a "normal" school.

What are some concerns of parents regarding the co-taught classroom?

Parents of students in solo and co-taught classes alike have similar concerns, about whether their child will be successful, enjoy learning, and have friends. Parents of general education students in the co-taught classroom worry about whether their children will be held back academically by having special education students in their class or whether discipline will be a problem. Parents of special education students wonder if their children will keep up with the rest of the students, be ostracized, improve their skills, and pass exams.

Co-teaching is designed to meet the needs of all students. With two teachers in the classroom simultaneously, the needs of every student can be met using various teaching strategies. Research reveals that parental perceptions of co-teaching classes are generally favorable (Tichenor et al., 2000), with typically achieving students doing well (Cole, Waldron, & Majd, 2004).

The co-taught classroom can create a positive climate of high expectations and high achievement for all students (Murawski & Diecker, 2004) and provide opportunities to expand learning for the most gifted students and those most at risk. Co-teachers can customize learning for the wide diversity of learners by intensifying and assessing learning using parallel, station, and alternative teaching.

Which co-teacher does the parent of a special education student contact?

Parents can contact either co-teacher. The advantage of a co-taught class is that the teachers plan lessons, set goals, and monitor student progress together;

therefore, either teacher is able to answer any parent concern. However, parents sometimes feel more comfortable talking with one teacher as opposed to another, so co-teaching enables parents to choose a teacher to communicate with and have their questions answered. Parental input is a valuable tool in any teaching situation because parents may identify a problem before the problem or concern manifests itself in the classroom. Successful co-teachers welcome and encourage parent input and communication, and they know their students well, enabling both of them to give parents an accurate description of the student's work and effort.

What kind of homework demands are appropriate for students in a co-taught inclusive class?

As for any other class, homework is assigned and students are responsible for its completion. Parents sometimes find homework to be a cause of disruptions in their home, with constant bickering over when and where the homework gets done. In a co-taught class, the homework that is assigned should either reinforce that day's lessons or lay the groundwork for the lesson to come the next day. The co-teachers may assign personalized homework based on what each child can handle independently. If homework becomes a problem for the student, the parent should contact the co-teachers to assess what is being assigned and to discuss the problems the student has with completing the assignment. If homework buddies are formally assigned, students can call a buddy to discuss or do the homework together.

According to Lacina-Gifford and Gifford (2004), "The only way to end the battle [over homework] is to make sure that homework is relevant, varied and takes place outside of the classroom" (p. 280). Co-teachers who spend time planning, modifying, and creating homework assignments that make use of the 21st century tools that students skillfully use and enjoy (e.g., computer, Internet, cell phones) have a better chance of creating meaningful and appropriate assignments. For example, an 8th grade co-taught English class in the United States connected with an 8th grade English class in Japan. These students became 21st century pen pals, writing autobiographies and sharing descriptive essays; as a result, their work was authentic and meaningful. A private elementary school had students use Twitter to tweet as characters from *Animal Farm*. Students logged onto their computers and used their 140 characters to tweet, taking the point of view of one of the characters in the book. For this homework assignment, students were motivated and learned how to research a character online. Each student wrote at his or her own pace and ability level and could be successful (Gorry, 2010).

Should parents of children with special needs join both SEPTA and PTA?

To be truly involved in the education of their children with special needs, parents need to know the issues of both general and special education students. Through the Special Education Parent Teacher Association (SEPTA) and Parent Teacher Association (PTA), parents of children with special needs can learn from other parents and find assistance with educational challenges. As a resource for parents, the PTA and SEPTA (both organizations can be researched at www.pta.org) offer a treasure trove of information on important topics including student success, safety, diversity, funding, inclusion, bullying, homework, and health and wellness. As students with special needs are increasingly included in the general education classrooms, it may be time to evaluate whether there is a need for two different parent organizations. One strong parent organization to support all students seems like an idea whose time has come, but if both organizations are available, it makes sense to take advantage of the support of both.

Are students with special needs accepted by their peers in a co-teaching environment?

In the co-taught class, students learn to respect one another and, in the best classes, learn to accept and celebrate differences. With two classroom teachers and a well-planned lesson that meets the individual needs of each student, students learn to encourage one another to reach goals unheard of before co-teaching. In a three-year study of urban elementary students in co-taught classes, researchers found that the students developed academically and as a community (York-Barr, Ghere, & Sommerness, 2007).

Co-teaching uses strategies of peer tutoring that enable students to teach and encourage one another in the learning process. As the co-taught class is often divided into small groups, students begin to care about and look out for one another. In fact, the co-taught classroom is the perfect environment to teach about individual differences and gain respect for these differences and the challenges students face daily. Shore (2009) emphasizes the need for teachers to incorporate activities that encourage understanding of students' diversities. He advocates character education as an important component in every classroom, and especially in the co-taught class. Shore reminds co-teachers to set a good example with their own behavior. Since the co-taught classroom consists of a diverse population, many opportunities exist for co-teachers to teach an appreciation of and to celebrate student differences.

Are students with special needs stigmatized in inclusive classrooms?

Quite the contrary. Public education has long been criticized for the ostracizing effects of placing students with special needs in separate learning environments (York-Barr et al., 2007). In the past, students with disabilities were segregated in their own special education classrooms, buses, and sometimes schools. In a co-taught class, co-teachers have the power to affect the values and character of their students. Co-teachers can promote respect and act as ethical mentors by providing classroom discussions and guidance regarding acceptance of others (Lickona, 1992).

Although we agree with Friend and colleagues (2010), who cite the need for empirical evidence to support co-teaching, we have witnessed in many school districts that students receive individual academic assistance in authentic co-taught classrooms, whether it be enriched or remedial. Students do not wear labels and are integrated no matter their ability level. Today's inclusive setting provides an environment for all students to belong, as noted by a 5th grade English special education co-teacher:

Students in the self-contained class were always fighting among themselves. I'd compare it with sibling rivalry, since these students were together since 1st grade. The students became very familiar with one another and knew what buttons to push to drive the other student over the edge. The time that I used to spend disciplining students is now spent teaching and learning in the co-taught class. Good behavior is modeled by the general education students. All students are learning good character traits including acceptance and respect.

Co-teachers must be vigilant not to inadvertently destroy the inclusive and accepting potential of the co-taught class. Care must be taken to avoid seating arrangements that segregate students based on ability and to avoid having the special education co-teacher work exclusively with students with special needs at the "back table."

How are the needs of the general education students met in an inclusive setting?

The research of Cole and colleagues (2004) reveals that the needs of general education students are met in the inclusive setting when the two teachers are truly co-teaching. All students reap the benefits of two teachers and gain from the learning strategies that the co-teachers use to enhance the lessons, and they are relieved of the stigma that may be placed on those who need assistance to master a lesson. In a co-taught class, there is a greater opportunity for an increase in student participation and assessment by dividing the students into small groups, as co-teachers can easily ascertain which students understand and which students are having problems with a particular concept. Each and every student gets the level of assistance he or she needs, and assignments are differentiated. In addition, typically achieving students in co-taught classes have the opportunity to receive more individualized instruction than in a solo-taught class. For instance, in a co-taught 4th grade class of 24 students, students were divided into four heterogeneous rotating stations for a science lesson. In two independent stations, students chose from a series of tasks that ranged in difficulty level while each co-teacher conducted separate experiments at different stations. The station activity created maximum learning opportunities for every student.

In another instance, a 7th grade social studies class of 21 students (6 students with special needs and 15 typically achieving students) were all earning low grades and were finding the work difficult. By analyzing exam results, the co-teachers determined that difficulties centered on basic vocabulary. They implemented a vocabulary peer tutoring strategy (see Chapter 7). A few days later, the co-teachers retested the students. All students passed the second test. Using activities that involve peers working together helps to keep all students, especially social students, interested and engaged in learning (Kroeger & Kouche, 2006). Through the implementation of the peer tutoring, students began to care about one another, and every student became an integral part of the learning environment.

Further demonstrating the power of strategies implemented in a co-taught class is the example offered by Danny, a gifted 6th grade student who finishes his work in record-breaking time and immediately distracts other students from learning. To avert this behavior, the co-teachers created a peer-tutoring schedule for Danny. As he tutors other students having trouble with a concept that he has mastered, Danny feels important and appreciated by his classmates and his co-teachers. As the grades of the tutored students improve, Danny became a hero instead of a distraction. This scenario emphasizes the positive results of peer tutoring for all students in the co-taught classroom and shows how pairing struggling students with students more proficient in the subject matter benefits everyone. "By explaining what he or she knows, the skilled reader's comprehension is increased while the unskilled reader received support in a nonthreatening manner" (Kozen et al., 2006, p. 198).

What do students think of co-teaching?

Most students respond positively to the co-teaching model. Wilson and Michaels (2006) found positive student reactions in a survey of 346 co-taught secondary education students (127 students with disabilities and 219 general education students in grades 7–12). Their findings on students' perceptions of the co-taught setting revealed four major, positive themes:

- Availability of help—Individual support and assistance are readily available in the co-teaching class for all students in need.
- Structural supports—The structure of co-teaching allows for more flexible and diverse instructional approaches.
- Multiple perspectives and styles—Co-teaching enables learners to experience and benefit from the opinions, styles, and approaches of both teachers.
- Skills and grades—Co-teaching classes help students to develop more skill and get better grades. (p. 214)

Three major themes emerged regarding students' perceptions of drawbacks to co-teaching.

• Structural supports—The structure of co-teaching makes it difficult to get away with anything and may make students think that they are always being monitored.

• Multiple perspectives and styles—Learners may get confused and get different guidance and/or conflicting directions from the two teachers.

• Skills and grades—Co-teaching classes assign more work and have higher grading standards and expectations for students. (p. 216)

The positive student responses regarding co-teaching might in themselves benefit students. Kortering and Braziel (1999) found that when students with special needs liked their learning environment, they were more likely to succeed in school, stay in school, and graduate.

How do teachers respond when students ask why there are two teachers in the classroom?

We have heard many answers to this question, from short and witty, to detailed and philosophical. The best responses correlate to the age of the students:

• "We are going to have two teachers teaching this class and we are going to have more fun learning," said the co-teachers. Third graders accepted this answer, and no other questions were ever asked.

• "This class is so great, we [co-teachers] both wanted to be here" was sufficient for a 4th grade class.

• "Because we wanted to have more fun learning, this class is going to have two teachers!" said 2nd grade co-teachers.

• "We have lots to learn this year. We have two teachers so that we can better teach all of you, quickly and easily," explained 7th grade teachers, who received smiles in return.

• "We are going to have two teachers for this class in order for you to learn more and be active learners," said 8th grade co-teachers.

• "This class will be co-taught in order for your needs to be successfully met, whether you are advanced or remedial or somewhere in between," explained co-teachers, as they easily satisfied the curiosity of 11th grade English students.

Wischnowski, Salmon, and Eaton (2004) found that implementation of co-teaching in primary grades laid the foundation for all students to be successful learners. And, as students became used to the co-taught classroom, it became the norm to have two teachers in the classroom. In a school district that used the co-teaching model for six years, middle school co-teachers say they are no longer asked why there were two teachers in the classroom. The philosophy is that co-teaching is just what we do here and the students know it.

———————•●•———————

Case Study 19

How can we address parents and their potentially negative perceptions of an inclusive, co-taught class?

At Back to School Night, the parents were informed that their children were scheduled in a co-taught, inclusive class. Parents had no idea what this meant, other than there were special education students in this class. A few parents pulled their children out of the class, thinking that the inclusion class was going to interfere with their children's academic advancement.

Statement of the problem

Some parents felt a co-taught class was academically inferior to a solo-taught class.

Problem genesis

Lack of properly disseminating information about co-teaching to parents.

How the problem is being denied or addressed

Transferring students to a general education class is not addressing the problem.

Ways of promoting a positive outcome

• In the spring of the year before initiating co-teaching, administrators need to publicize the idea at PTA meetings, hold special information nights, and speak at Board of Education sessions to start educating the public on what co-teaching is, why they are doing it, and the results they hope to obtain.

• Some school districts have initiated co-teaching campaigns that explain the benefits of a co-taught class. After hearing one district's description of co-teaching, a parent said, "Why wouldn't you want your child in a co-taught class with two teachers to help?"

• Districts find that during the second year of co-teaching, parents of general education students want their children to continue in the co-taught class. That presents another problem for the school administration as they try to randomly select general education students to ensure a class balance of heterogeneous students.

• A parent who doesn't want his or her child in a co-taught class usually does not have an accurate understanding of co-teaching. Educators are not always the best promoters of their craft. The positive results of co-teaching need to be published and disseminated among all stakeholders.

Case Study 20

How do we explain why some students leave the classroom to take exams?

The students in the co-taught class seem happy to have two teachers. When asked, the students stated that their questions are always answered, there is someone to help when they need it, and they like having two different points of view on some topics. The one area that caused student concern related to quizzes and tests. The special education co-teacher takes the students who are classified out of the room whenever there is an exam. Some of the students with special needs don't want to leave the room, perhaps because they are embarrassed or think that they don't need to leave the room, but they are told that they have to go to a separate setting to be tested. The general education students don't know why some students leave the room and wonder if those students are getting more help to pass the exam.

Statement of the problem

Students have little understanding as to why some students take exams in a different setting.

Problem genesis

The teachers have made testing a secretive action by not openly explaining the testing process.

How the problem is being denied or addressed

The co-teachers are not explaining the testing process to the class, therefore some students feel jealous of other students.

Ways of promoting a positive outcome

• Co-teachers may ask all the students if they would like to take their exam in a quieter, smaller setting. Some students who do not have IEPs get easily distracted and would also benefit from a smaller testing setting. Co-teachers try to accommodate every student, whether classified or not. Students who feel they would do better in a quieter testing environment or seated in the front of the classroom or away from the window can always be accommodated.

• A brief description of the testing environment required by the particular set of students at the beginning of the year would end the testing mystique. Co-teachers can lead a class discussion on learning and testing strategies and ask students to write on an index card how they think they learn best and how they would describe their ideal testing situation.

• In a co-taught class, the teachers need to explain that the needs of all students are met, not just the needs of special education students. Co-teachers often use special education strategies to deliver lessons to all students, and each student can be accommodated by offering the best testing environment for him or her. When students feel they are being treated equally and sense no mysteries about testing or grading, then everyone can focus on learning and succeeding.

References

Note: Additional resources related to co-teaching are available online at www.ascd. org/books. Look under the sample files for this book.

Aldrich, S., & Wright, J. (2001). Curriculum-based assessment: Directions and materials. Retrieved July 11, 2011, from http://www.programevaluation.org/docs/ cbamanall.pdf

Allington, R. L. (2002). You can't learn from books you can't read. *Educational Leadership, 60*(3), 16–19.

Aud, S., Hussar, W., Kena, G. Bianco, K., Frohlich, L., Kemp, J., & Tahan, K. (2011). *The condition of education 2011* (NCES 2011-033). U.S. Department of Education, National Center for Education Statistics, Washington, DC: Goverment Printing Office.

Austin, V. (2001). Teachers' beliefs about co-teaching. *Remedial and Special Education, 22*(4), 245–255.

Bowe, F. (2006). *Disability in America*. Hempstead, NY: Hofstra University.

Bowen, S. K., & Rude, H. A. (2006). Assessment and students with disabilities: Issues and challenges with educational reform. *Rural Special Education Quarterly, 25*(3), 24–30.

Buehl, D. (2009). *Classroom strategies for interactive learning*. Newark, DE: International Reading Association.

Center for Applied Science Technology (CAST). (2008). *Universal Design for Learning guidelines version 1.0*. Wakefield, MA: Author.

Chopra, R. V., & French, N. K. (2004). Paraeducator relationships with parents of students with significant disabilities. *Remedial and Special Education, 25*(4), 240–251.

Cole, C. M., Waldron, N., & Majd, M. (2004). Academic progress of students across inclusive and traditional settings. *Mental Retardation, 47*(2), 136–144.

Cook, L., & Friend, M. (1995). Co-teaching: Guidelines for creating effective practices. *Focus on Exceptional Children, 28*(3), 1–16.

Cooper, H. (2001). *The battle over homework: Common ground for administrators, teachers, and parents*. Thousand Oaks, CA: Corwin.

Davis, L. L., & O'Neil, R. E. (2004). Use of response cards with a group of students with learning disabilities including those for whom English is a second language. *Journal of Applied Behavior Analysis, 37*(2), 210–222. Retrieved March 7, 2011, from http://www.ncbi.nlm.nih.gov/pmc/articles/PMC1284497/pdf/15293641.pdf

Deshler, D. D. (n.d.). A closer look: Closing the performance gap. Retrieved from Alliance for Excellence in Education website: http://www.all4ed.org/files/ACloserLook.pdf

Donhost, M., & Hoover, R. (2007, September/October). Creating change through staff development. *Leadership, 37*(1), pp. 28–38.

Ellis, E. S. (1997). Watering up the curriculum for adolescents with learning disabilities. *Remedial & Special Education, 18*(6), 326–346.

Ellis, E. S. (2003). *The LINCS vocabulary strategy*. Lawrence, KS: Edge Enterprises.

Ellis, E. S. (2008). *The framing routine*. Lawrence, KS: Edge Enterprises.

Ellis, E. S., & Worthington, L. A. (1994). *Effective teaching principles and the design of quality tools for educators*. Technical report no. 5. National Center to Improve the Tools of Educators, 1–108.

Freedman, M. K. (2000). *Testing, grading, and granting diplomas to special education students*. (Special Report No. 18). Horsham, PA: LRP Publications.

Freedman, M. K. (2005). *Student testing and the law: The requirements educators, parents, and officials should know*. Horsham, PA: LRP Publications.

French, N. K., & Chopra, R. B. (1999). Parent perspectives on the roles of paraprofessionals. *Journal of the Association for Persons with Severe Handicaps (JASH), 24*(4), 259–272.

Friend, M., Cook, L., Hurley-Chamberlain, D., & Shamberger, C. (2010). Co-teaching: An illustration of the complexity of collaboration in special education. *Journal of Educational and Psychological Consultation,* 20, 9–27.

Friend, M., & Hurley-Chamberlain, D. (n.d.). Is co-teaching effective? [Online article]. Available at http://www.cec.sped.org/AM/Template.cfm?Section=home&TEMPLATE=/CM/contentdisplay.cfm&CONTENTID=7504

Fritschmann, N. S., Deshler, D. D., & Schumaker, J. B. (2007). The effects of instruction in an inference strategy on reading comprehension skills of adolescents with disabilities. *Learning Disability Quarterly, 30*(4), 245–262.

Fuchs, D., Fuchs, L. S., & Burish, P. (2000). Peer assisted learning strategies: An evidence-based practice to promote reading achievement. *Learning Disabilities Research & Practice, 15*(2), 85–91.

Gately, S. E., & Gately, F. J. (2001). Understanding coteaching components. *Teaching Exceptional Children, 33*(4), 40–47.

Giangreco, M. F. (2010). One-to-one paraprofessionals for students with disabilities in inclusive classrooms: Is conventional wisdom wrong? *Intellectual and Developmental Disabilities, 48*(1), 1–13.

Giangreco, M. F., Edelman, S. W., Luiselli, T. E., & MacFarland, S. Z. C. (1997). Helping or hovering? Effects of instructional assistant proximity on students with disabilities. *Exceptional Children, 64*(1), 7–18.

Gloeckler, L. C. (2001). The door to opportunity: Let's open it for everyone. *State Education Standard, 2,* 21–25.

Goldhammer, K. (1983). Evolution in the profession. *Educational Administration Quarterly, 19,* 249–272.

Gorry, M. (2010, May 5). Students share school Twitter project at city conference. *Long Island Catholic,* p. 9.

Hoener, A., Salend, S., & Kay, S. (1997). Creating readable handouts, worksheets, overheads, tests, review materials, study guides, and homework assignments through effective typographic design. *Teaching Exceptional Children, 29*(3), 33–35.

Individuals with Disabilities Education Improvement Act of 2004, Pub. L. 108-446, 118 Stat. 2647. (2004). Retrieved May 10, 2011, from http://www.copyright.gov/legislation/pl108-446.pdf

Jung, L. A., & Guskey, T. R. (2010). Grading exceptional learners. *Educational Leadership, 67*(5), 31–35.

Kortering, J., & Braziel, P. (1999). School dropout from the perception of former students: Implications for secondary special education programs. *Remedial and Special Education, 20*(2), 78–83.

Kozen, A. A., Murray, R. K., & Windell, I. (2006). Increasing all students' chance to achieve: Using and adapting anticipation guides with middle school learners. *Intervention in School and Clinic, 41*(4), 195–200.

Kroeger, S. D., & Kouche, B. (2006). Using peer-assisted learning strategies to increase response to intervention in inclusive middle math settings. *Council for Exceptional Children, 38*(5), 6–13.

Lacina-Gifford, L. J., & Gifford, R. B. (2004). Putting an end to the battle over homework. *Education, 125*(2), 279–281.

Lee, S., Amos, B., Gragoudas, S., Lee, Y., Shogren, K., Theoharis, R., & Wehmeyer, M. (2006). Curriculum augmentation and adaptation strategies to promote access to the general curriculum for students with intellectual and developmental disabilities. *Education and Training in Developmental Disabilities, 41*(3), 199–212.

Lenz, B. K., Deshler, D. D., & Kissam, B. R. (2004). *Teaching content to all: Evidence-based inclusive practices in middle and secondary schools.* Upper Saddle River, NJ : Pearson.

Lenz, B. K., & Hughes, C. A. (1990). A word identification strategy for adolescents with learning disabilities. *Journal of Learning Disabilities, 23*, 149–158.

Lenz, B. K., Schumaker, J. B., Deshler, D. D., & Beals, V. L. (1984). *The word identification strategy.* Lawrence, KS: University of Kansas.

Lickona, T. (1992). *Educating for character: How our schools can teach respect and responsibility.* New York: Bantam Books.

Magiera, K., & Zigmond, N. (2005). Co-teaching in middle school classrooms under routine conditions: Does the instructional experience differ for students with disabilities in co-taught and solo-taught classes? *Learning Disabilities Research & Practice, 20*(2), 79–85.

Master, K. (2006). Research on peer-assisted learning strategies: The promise and limitations of peer mediated instruction. *Reading & Writing Quarterly, 22*(1), 5–25.

McKenzie, R. G. (2009). A national survey of pre-service preparation for collaboration. *Teacher Education and Special Education, 32*(4), 379–393.

McMaster, K. L., Fuchs, D., & Fuchs, L. S. (2006). Research on peer-assisted learning strategies: The promise and limitations of peer mediated instruction. *Reading & Writing Quarterly, 22*(1), 5–25.

Murawski, W. (2010). *Collaborative teaching in elementary schools: Making the co-teaching marriage work!* Thousand Oaks, CA: Corwin.

Murawski, W., & Hughes, C. (2009). Response to intervention, collaboration and co-teaching: A logical combination for successful systemic change. *Preventing School Failure, 54*(4), 268–277.

Murawski, W. W., & Dieker, L. A. (2004). Tips and strategies for co-teaching at the secondary level. *Teaching Exceptional Children, 36*(5), 52–58.

Murawski, W. W., & Swanson, H. L. (2001). The meta-analysis of co-teaching research: Where are the data? *Remedial and Special Education, 22*(4), 258–267.

New York State Education Department. (2006). *Overview of teaching assistant certification requirements* (effective April 2006). Retrieved May 20, 2011, from http://www.highered.nysed.gov/tcert/career/ta.html

Office of Civil Rights. (2008, October 17). *Dear colleague letter: Report card and transcripts for students with disabilities.* Available: www.ed.gov/about/offices/list/ocr/letters/colleague-20081017.html

Primo, A. T. (1972). *Willowbrook: The last great disgrace* [DVD]. Available from https://sproutflix.org.

Ring, M. M., & Rietz, L. (2000). Modification effects on attribution of middle school students with learning disabilities, *Learning Disabilities Research and Practice, 15*, 34–42.

Rothstein, A., Rothstein, E., & Lauber, G. (2006). *Writing as learning: A content-based approach* (2nd ed.). Thousand Oaks, CA: Corwin.

Schumaker, J. B., Denton, P. H., & Deshler, D. D. (1984). *The paraphrasing strategy.* Lawrence, KS: University of Kansas.

Schumm, J., Vaughn, S., & Leavell, A. (1994). Planning pyramid: A framework for planning for diverse needs during content instruction. *The Reading Teacher, 47*(8), 608–615.

Scruggs, T., Mastropieri, M., & McDuffie, K. (2007). Co-teaching in inclusive classrooms: A metasynthesis of qualitative research. *Exceptional Children, 73*(4), 392–416.

Shore, K. (2009). Preventing bullying: Nine ways to bully-proof your classroom. *Education Digest, 75*(4), 39–44.

Siebold, T. (2008). *Collegial circles.* Retrieved May 5, 2011, from http://www.teacherssontarget.com/Collegial%20Circles.htm

Simmons, D. C., & Kame'enui, E. J. (1996). A focus on curriculum design: When children fail. *Focus on Exceptional Children, 28*(7), 1–16.

Snyder, T. D. & Dillow, S. A. (2010). *Digest of education statistics 2009* (NCES 2010-013). National Center for Education Statistics, Institute of Education Sciences, U.S. Department of Education, Washington, DC: Government Printing Office.

Soukup, J., Wehmeyer, M., Bashinski, S., & Bovaird, J. (2007). Classroom variables and access to the general curriculum for students with disabilities. *Exceptional Children, 74*(1), 101–120.

Thompson, S. J., & Thurlow, M. L. (2001). Participation of students with disabilities in state assessment systems. *Assessment for Effective Intervention, 26*(2), 5–8.

Tichenor, M. S., Heins, B., & Piechura-Couture, K. (2000). Parent perceptions of a co-taught inclusive classroom. *Education, 120*(3), 569–574.

U.S. Department of Education. (2005, June 21). Qualifications for teachers and paraprofessionals, Section 1119. Retrieved July 11, 2011, from http://www2.ed.gov/policy/elsec/leg/esea02/pg2.html#se

U.S. Department of Education. (2007). History: Twenty-five years of progress in educating children with disabilities through IDEA. Retrieved March 7, 2011, from http://www2.ed.gov/policy/speced/leg/idea/history.html

Vaughn, S., Schumm, S., Shay, J., & Arguelles, M. E., (1997). The ABCDEs of co-teaching. *Teaching Exceptional Children, 30*(2), 4–11.

Walsh, J. M., & Jones, B. (2004). New models of cooperative teaching. *Teaching Exceptional Children, 36*(5) 14–20.

Walther-Thomas, C., & Bryant, M. (1996). Planning for effective co-teaching. *Remedial and Special Education, 17*(4), 255–264.

Will, M. C. (1986, February). Educating children with learning problems: A shared responsibility. *Exceptional Children, 52*(5), 411–414. Retrieved March 31, 2011, from http://www.mnddc.org/parallels2/pdf/80s/86/86-ECP-MCW.pdf

Wilson, G. L. (2005). This doesn't look familiar! A supervisor's guide for observing co-teachers. *Intervention in School and Clinic, 40*(5), 271–275.

Wilson, G. L. (2007). Seeing the forest and the trees. Understanding the big ideas and details through the concept format model. *Insights in Learning Disabilities, 4*(1), 1–12.

Wilson, G. L., Kim, S. A., & Michaels, C. A. (prepublished June 20, 2011). Factors associated with where secondary students with disabilities are educated and how they are doing. *The Journal of Special Education.* DOI: 10.1177/0022466911411575.

Wilson, G. L., & Michaels, C. A. (2006). General and special education students' perceptions of co-teaching: Implications for secondary-level literacy instruction. *Reading & Writing Quarterly, 22*(3), 205–225.

Wischnowski, M. W., Salmon, S. J., & Eaton, K. (2004). Evaluation co-teaching as a means for successful inclusion of students with disabilities in a rural district. *Rural Special Education Quarterly, 23*(3), 3–14.

Wolfensburger, W. (1972). *The principle of normalization in human services.* Toronto: National Institute on Mental Retardation.

Wright, J. (n.d.). Curriculum-based measurement: A manual for teachers. Retrieved July 11, 2011, from http://www.jimwrightonline.com/pdfdocs/cbaManual.pdf.

York-Barr, J., Ghere, G., & Sommerness, J. (2007). Collaborative teaching to increase ELL student learning: A three-year urban elementary case study. *Journal of Education for Students Placed at Risk, 12*(3), 301–335.

Ysseldyke, J., Nelson, J. R., Christenson, S., Johnson, D. R., Dennison, A., Triezenberg, H., Sharpe, M., & Hawes, M. (2004). What we know and need to know about the consequences of high-stakes testing for students with disabilities. *Exceptional Children, 71*, 75–95.

Zigmond, N. (2001). Special education at a crossroads. *Preventing School Failure, 45*(2), 70–75.

Index

Note: The letter *f* following a page number denotes a figure.

About the Authors

 **Gloria Lodato Wilson** is associate professor and director of special education programs in the Department of Counseling, Rehabilitation, Special Education and Research at Hofstra University, New York. She received her doctorate from New York University. Wilson is the author of numerous articles on co-teaching and learning strategies, and her research focuses on inclusive settings, particularly the effectiveness of co-taught programs and associated teaching strategies. As a consultant to school districts, Wilson provides professional development workshops and coaching to administrators, co-teachers, and paraprofessionals. Having taught in public and private settings from preschool to higher education as a speech and language therapist, special education teacher, and professor for 37 years, she is committed to translating research into effective practices in today's classrooms. She may be contacted at gloria.wilson@hofstra.edu.

 **Joan Blednick** has more than 40 years' experience in public education, as a teacher, guidance counselor, administrator, and adjunct college professor. She received her doctorate in education from Nova University. Most recently, as principal of the Ames Campus of Massapequa High School, New York, Blednick developed and implemented a co-teaching model. Presently, as an educational consultant for Strategic Training and Research Consultants in New York, she strives to build effective co-teaching programs. The scope of Blednick's experience in education has helped her understand how all the parts work best together in an integrated model of co-teaching. She may be contacted at jabled@optonline.net.